BALANCING ACT

THE POLITICAL ROLE
OF THE URBAN SCHOOL
SUPERINTENDENT

BARBARA L. JACKSON

JOINT CENTER FOR POLITICAL AND ECONOMIC STUDIES
WASHINGTON, D.C.

The Joint Center for Political and Economic Studies is a national, nonprofit institution that conducts research on public policy issues of special concern to black Americans and promotes informed and effective involvement of blacks in the governmental process. Founded in 1970, the Joint Center provides independent and nonpartisan analyses through research, publication, and outreach programs.

Copyright 1995 by the Joint Center for Political and Economic Studies, Inc.
1090 Vermont Avenue, NW, Suite 1100
Washington, D.C. 20005-4961

Distributed by arrangement with
University Press of America
4720 Boston Way
Lanham, MD 20706

3 Henrietta Street
London WC2E 8LU England

Library of Congress Cataloging-in-Publication Data
Jackson, Barbara L. (Barbara Loomis), 1928–
    Balancing act : the political role of the urban school superintendent /
    Barbara L. Jackson.
        p.   cm.
    Includes bibliographical references and index.
    ISBN 0-8191-9562-6 (cloth : alk. paper). —ISBN 0-8191-9563-4
(pbk. : alk. paper)
        1. School superintendents—United States. 2. Education, Urban—Political
aspects—United States. 3. Education and state—United States. 4. School
management and organization—United States.
I. Title.
LB2831.72.J33   1996
371.2 011—dc20   95-39456
                                                                          CIP

ISBN 0-8191-9562-6 (cloth: alk paper)
ISBN 0-8191-9563-4 (pbk.: alk paper)

FOREWORD

In today's society, a good education is one of the most important investments we can make in our children. Indeed, for many black children, a solid foundation of basic schooling may offer the only escape from a path that otherwise heads toward hopelessness. However, the current instability in school governance is threatening to close off that escape route. In urban school systems across the country, this instability is manifested in the alarmingly high turnover among superintendents. Their tenure now averages only two to three years. Such instability in urban superintendencies brings with it an almost constant change in management goals and procedures that can be quite destructive, weakening the hope of meaningful school reform and progress in student achievement.

Political conflict contributes to the controversy that makes the tenure of school superintendents as short as it is today. Recent experiences in Detroit, Cleveland, Chicago, and New York City illustrate this. Yet politics is not entirely a negative force. In an open, democratically governed society, political influence is a factor that makes public schooling more responsive to the needs of the citizenry.

In this book, Barbara Jackson describes the evolution of the superintendency, tracing the growing influence of politics on this position. She provides a rare historical perspective that reveals how this public office has been transformed over the decades by the broader changes in our society. Her analysis of current issues, including multicultural curricula and the racially charged politics of city-versus-suburb, sheds light on the balancing act school officials routinely perform today. Dr. Jackson tells us why superintendents must learn how to cope with their political role, and suggests as well how they can do so in constructive ways. For newer and aspiring superintendents, school boards, and indeed anyone interested in the state of urban education, this book should be an invaluable primer.

The book was commissioned as part of Superintendents Prepared, a collaborative program of the Joint Center, the Institute for Educational

Leadership, and the McKenzie Group. This consortium program has been supported for the past three years by the Rockefeller, Prudential, and Ford foundations, the Pew Charitable Trusts, the DeWitt Wallace-Reader's Digest Fund, and Citibank. The purpose of the initiative is to help individuals become more effective leaders in urban schools. We are very pleased to be able to bring this publication to the public.

I would especially like to thank Dr. Milton Morris, the Joint Center's vice president for research, for his direction and guidance in producing this work. I would also like to acknowledge my colleagues in this joint effort, Dr. Floretta McKenzie of the McKenzie Group and Michael Usdan, president of the Institute for Educational Leadership, for their wisdom on issues of educational governance.

Eddie N. Williams
President
Joint Center for Political and Economic Studies

Contents

LIST OF TABLES AND FIGURES

About the Author

Barbara L. Jackson, professor of education at Fordham University's Graduate School of Education, has been an educator and scholar for more than three decades. She received her doctorate in education from Harvard University. Among her previous appointments, she served as dean of the School of Education at Morgan State University. She has also directed evaluation at the National Urban League Street Academy, and currently cochairs the Boston-based Institute for Responsive Education. Dr. Jackson's articles have appeared in numerous journals, including *Urban Education, College Teaching, Initiatives,* and *the Politics of Education Association Yearbook.* In 1995, Dr. Jackson received the Kathryn I. Scanlon Award from the Fordham University School of Education Alumni Association for her significant contributions to education.

Author's Acknowledgments

My thanks and appreciation to those who shared their ideas with me about the general topic of urban politics and the political role of the superintendent in particular, especially Michael Usdan, Betty Hale, Barbara McCloud, Milton Bins, and LaRuth Gray. My participation in the seminar for the Superintendents Prepared Program under the leadership of Floretta McKenzie provided an opportunity to hear and talk with outstanding speakers and participants as well as test out some of the ideas that formed the basis for this book. In addition, I am grateful to the educators who granted me interviews at the beginning of my research, especially former superintendents Deborah McGriff in Detroit and Lois Harrison Jones in Boston.

My appreciation is extended to Milton Morris and Margaret Simms of the Joint Center for giving me this opportunity to extend my research on educational politics; to Carrie Robinson, Barbara McCloud, and Bruce Cooper, who read early drafts and shared their comments; and finally to Marc DeFrancis, senior editor at the Joint Center, for his patience and continuing support during the many months of editing.

—B.J.

CHAPTER 1

THE DIMENSIONS OF THE SUPERINTENDENCY

Since its inception 150 years ago, the role of the superintendent of public schools has undergone many changes. From a small beginning as clerk of the school committee or board of education hired primarily to coordinate a school's day-to-day operations, the position has steadily grown in responsibility and status. Today it can still be said, as the National Education Association's Educational Policies Commission wrote in 1965, that

> the superintendency of schools is one of the most crucial and perhaps most difficult public positions in American life today. The occupant of this position, more than any other single person in the community, influences the shape of public education. Thus he has a basic role in determining what will become of the young people of his community, and through them what his community and the nation will become.[1]

A variety of factors have been responsible for shaping the current superintendent's role. They include the internal operation of the schools, which has changed over the years; social, economic, political, and legal forces external to the schools; professors of educational administration who prepare those seeking the superintendency; the expectations and values of the public; and finally, the individuals themselves who have held the office, including their perceptions of the job, their views of the role of public schools in American society, and their own backgrounds, values, and personalities.

As educational scholar Arthur Blumberg writes, "the superintendency today, if it is to be an effective office, must be conceived of in political terms, if by that we mean the ability of the incumbent to work with a wide array of conflicting forces so as to maintain the delicate balance upon which the vitality of school life depends."[2] While a political dimension has always existed, the problems facing the schools today suggest that the political role needs rethinking. The superintendent's role has evolved into one that is multidimensional and often ambiguous.

For today's superintendent, the expectations and constituencies are many, requiring a balancing act between internal and external forces over which he or she has little control. Often events are unpredictable. The position's political side is complicated by the public's views about the importance of education, the relation of schools to the political process, and the reputation of politicians. The school superintendency is similar to other executive positions in that it carries responsibility for managing what may be a multimillion-dollar enterprise. Finally, while the position's public role resembles that of other public officials, there is a significant difference: the superintendent is also perceived as a teacher, scholar, and leader—a professional expert—and in addition is viewed by many as the guardian of the community's children. The three major roles of executive, public official, and politician deserve special attention.

Role as Executive/Manager

The superintendent of schools has responsibilities similar to those of any executive or business manager. Even though some systems are so small that the superintendent is the only central office staff member (and may have to fill in as a substitute teacher or even drive the school bus), all superintendents have some managerial responsibilities. In small towns as well as large cities, the school system is often a major employer, so personnel policies and practices must be written and staff development programs designed. Budgets must be negotiated and managed. Accountability for funds is a critical responsibility, one that has led to the downfall of many superintendents (and some school board members). All systems have public buildings that must be maintained, and new ones must be planned and built. Superintendents, like their counterparts in any business, are expected to provide for and direct the institution they lead so that it can reach its goals, ambiguous and conflicting as they may be; to set in motion procedures to resolve conflicts; and to pay attention to both the internal and external environments upon which the welfare of the organization depends.3

During the period at the beginning of this century when so-called scientific management reigned—when business methods were adopted by schools—superintendents (and the institutions that prepared them) saw this managerial role as paramount, almost to the exclusion of anything else. Too often, superintendents looked only *inside* the schools, which were regarded as closed systems.

For all the similarities to the managerial role of the business executive, the superintendent has a unique responsibility. Executives of American Express or IBM or Ford may come under attack for not producing a quality product, but that criticism is nothing compared to what may be said about a superintendent and the school system when they fail to live up to a community's expectations. School leaders are guardians of a sacred public trust, the community's most precious possessions—its children. Unlike the business executive, the superintendent has numerous constituencies to please—students, parents, teachers, principals, the community, and most important, the school board. This is where the superintendent's role as public official and politician comes into play.

Role as Public Official

The superintendent's role may also be viewed as that of a public official. The superintendent is classified as a public official since he or she is paid from public funds, but the position differs from that of most other officials in important respects. Most officials are elected for a specific term and cannot be fired without a complicated impeachment process.4 They are accepted as partisan politicians with a constituency to whom they can and do turn for support—their political parties.

Superintendents, on the other hand, are nonelected employees (except in a few Southern states that still have elected superintendents). They are appointed by school boards and usually serve at the boards' pleasure, contracts notwithstanding. It is now well established that if a board fires the superintendent before the end of the contract, the school system must pay the balance. Because superintendents are not directly elected, they have no formal constituency for support but must cultivate both the board and the community through their own efforts. Unpopular decisions on their part often lead to their dismissal.

The position is similar to that of a city manager in that both officials are professional experts responsible to a lay elected board or council. Few big cities, however, have the city-manager form of government; most have a strong mayor–city-council form where elected officials are full-time paid employees. In dealing with the school boards and mayors, superintendents have always faced conflicts and dilemmas. In the report of their 1985 pilot study, L. Harmon Zeigler, Ellen Nehoe, and Jane Reisman state:

> Traditional democratic theory holds that political influence ought to follow lines of legal authority. Administrators in school districts and city governments should follow the instructions of their constituents (the public). Boards of education and city councils appoint superintendents and city managers and may remove them when they so desire. Superintendents and city managers are administrative officers responsive to legislatures which in turn are accountable to the public.[5]

Therein lies the dilemma: who is accountable for the results of schooling? Who controls the decisions? If the "public" is dissatisfied with the outcomes, does it remove the school board, the superintendent, or both?

Once schooling had become more complex, reflecting an ever more industrial and technological world, the school board had to rely on the professional expertise of the administrator. Board members believed that these people could be both politically neutral and technically competent.[6] But while citizens may accept claims of expertise in education, they may not completely accept the expert when it comes to the values they want promoted. Indeed, many decisions affecting the education of children cannot be based solely on technical, professional knowledge. How do conflicting values in a community get resolved? Stephen Bailey and his coauthors suggest that the answer lies in politics, in the "fashioning of coalitions of influence in an attempt to determine what values will be authoritatively implemented by government."[7]

The word "values" illustrates how politics is both a necessary and useful process for schools. In a pluralistic society where respecting differences among people and groups is itself a widely accepted value, it follows that the ends—the common good, the public interest—will, by definition, be multiple and often conflicting. In reality, many publics exist with the right to have their point of view considered as the basis for determining the common good and the allocation of resources. The pluralism of American society is nowhere more evident than in the arena of public education.

Since the 1960s, the conflict over which values should be the basis for school programs and other educational services has intensified. Education scholar Robert Crowson, who sees the administrator as crucial in addressing the issue of values, writes:

> In brief summary, a decoding of political messages begins and ends with questions of value. When elites are in control or there is a close integration of values within a community, the administrator is likely to consider a narrow range of codes. As the political system adds separate and sometimes conflicting interests, the educator's own values become more and more salient: To whom and to what do I owe first allegiance?[8]

Is the superintendent simply to be guided by the dominant values of the school community? Crowson suggests that the mission of the school may have to go beyond socialization or supporting the authority of parents to promote their values. Do schools, he asks, have an "enlightenment function," that is, a duty to develop in students a capacity to become moral agents and to develop a voice of conscience beyond either family or community values? In answering this question, Crowson quotes political scientist Amy Gutman: "To prevent education from being repressive, we must defend a principled limit on both political and parental authority, a limit that in practice requires parents and governments to cede some educational authority to professional educators."9 If part of the purpose of schooling is to change society as well as perpetuate it, school leaders may need to rethink the goals of schools and their own values.

Superintendents are the most visible exponents of education in the community. They are "public property," to use Arthur Blumberg's term.10 They are seen as accessible to any and all—visible and vulnerable as perhaps no other public official is (except perhaps the mayor, especially a black mayor). Visibility often limits the private lives of superintendents. Those accepting this position as a special kind of public servant must be willing to do what is required and expected by their various constituencies.

Role as Politician

While the superintendent's role as executive/manager and public servant have been regarded as legitimate and appropriate, his role as politician has not. One reason for this is the still-prevalent idea that schools should not be involved in politics; another reason hinges on the way politicians are viewed.

Public schools are, in fact, caught up in politics. Local school boards are elected or appointed by elected officials, frequently by the mayor. Schools are supported by taxes on citizens and their property and by funds appropriated by federal and state governments. The decisions these governing bodies make about the schools are inevitably political decisions.

A major responsibility of government is to manage conflict. "Many students of government believe that, whatever else they may think they are doing, governors govern by managing conflict," writes Zeigler (*et al.*) in his 1985 report, adding, "They institutionalize it, mobilize it, channel it into appropriate directions, ignore it, outlast it, or suppress it. The job of government is to handle conflict."11 Because public schools are part of a politically governed system, management of conflict must necessarily become a normal part of the superintendent's job. As Frank Lutz and Carol Merz write, "School districts are political organizations. Conflict will occur. The question is when, to what degree, and how it will be handled. Any notion that consensus and harmony comprise the natural state of a dynamic, changing, and heterogeneous political system like a school district harbors the seeds of unrealistic expectations and is sure to spawn discontent and disappointment."[12]

Given that schools are political organizations in a democratic society, the superintendent, as educational leader and executive to the lay board of education, which represents the will of the people, must keep in mind the political element of his or her role. According to Robert Peterkin, former superintendent in both Cambridge, Massachusetts, and Milwaukee, Wisconsin, the superintendent needs to be political but should not be partisan. The 1985 report by Zeigler (*et al.*) makes the same point clearly: "Contrary to the professional maxim that they should not engage in politics, superintendents are political actors with political powers. As with other units of government, school district governance involves conflict."[13] The coauthors of that report found that dealing with conflict creates a paradox for the superintendent that may not exist for the city manager:

> For many superintendents, political conflict presents a crucial paradox; when conflict occurs, the technical skills so diligently developed are not only useless, they are a liability. Trained in the tenets of an ideology that defines conflict as pathological and consensus as the most legitimate basis for decisions, super-intendents may find conflict more painful than other executive officers. A defensive, hostile response to criticism may then generate more intensive conflict.[14]

Superintendents have never been totally apolitical. What has changed is the way in which they have exercised that part of their role in response to changing conditions.

CHAPTER 2

HISTORY AND EVOLUTION OF THE SUPERINTENDENCY

The evolution of the role of the public school superintendent has paralleled the growth of the nation and reflected changing social, economic, and political conditions. Schools and school leaders have also influenced these conditions. Our schools evolved from educating only the privileged class to educating the children of the common man, preparing students for occupations in every field, and as this happened the nation itself was transformed. In the published histories of education, however, not much attention has been given to this reciprocal influence.[15] The brief history outlined in this chapter embraces two broad stages of development that are frequently treated separately in the historical literature: from the colonial period to 1940, and from 1940 until 1970. The current period, whose political landscape was transformed by the civil rights movement and the Voting Rights Act that it led to, is covered in the chapter that follows.

Early Developments

The prime motivation for the colonists' interest in schooling was not the education of the individual as such but rather religion and Bible reading—at least in the New England settlements. The schools were seen as supporting the values taught at home. It was not until later that schools were seen as instruments for developing the nation and preparing individuals to be citizens; this required that they promote the values associated with the Protestant ethic, including working hard, separating work from play, and preparing for the future. The very nature of the

American experiment in democracy, however, meant that conflict over values would persist.

Most historians cite 1642 as the beginning of public education; it was then that the first schools were established in the towns of Massachusetts. For most of the colonial period, committees in each local community operated their schools directly. Eventually they found that help was needed to coordinate the schools' day-to-day operations, and they hired clerks. The clerks, however, were given little responsibility for directing the curriculum or the teaching staff.

As the need for money increased, the state government, whose power to tax was greater than the local communities', assumed more control. With funding came regulation to account for the monies—a function that was to expand over the centuries.

The pressures on schools to expand their role intensified with the influx of immigrants in the second half of the nineteenth century. The immigrants, who came primarily from Europe, had to be "Americanized" and taught citizenship. With these added responsibilities and growing numbers of students, school boards, while continuing to determine policies, looked to the "clerk" to assume a new role—that of teacher and scholar. For the first time, ambiguity arose as to who would be responsible for defining a school's purpose and for planning and carrying out its programs, the professional expert or the lay volunteer board representing the public. The same conflict has erupted periodically ever since.

Most historians cite Buffalo, New York, as the first city to employ a superintendent, which it did in the year 1837. By the 1870s, most big cities had such a position, as did many smaller communities. Most states also had a state superintendent, in many cases having created this position before the towns and cities established theirs.

The political role of the superintendent may not have been emphasized in this early period, but at least one incumbent is quoted as having said in 1883: "The work of a superintendent is also political in its character. He ought to be a politician." Apparently this official was not advocating that a superintendent engage in partisan politics or be a politician "in the common acceptation of that term" but rather that he be "one versed in the science of government."[16]

As the twentieth century began, America was rapidly changing from an agrarian and small-town society to an industrial, urbanized nation. New demands were put on the schools to prepare young people for this new world. The schools were profoundly affected at this time by two movements in society: Frederick Taylor's "scientific management" approach to industrial operations and the good-government reform movement. The schools responded, and in the process the role of the superintendent changed.

The term "cult of efficiency," coined by educational scholar Raymond Callahan, aptly describes the widespread belief during that period that schools should be run like factories. The term refers to two interrelated ideas: the definition of the superintendent as professional expert and the creation of a business-oriented bureaucracy responsible for educating the growing and increasingly diverse population. These ideas merged in the 1920s with the good-government movement, which sought to eliminate the corruption and patronage that often permeated municipal government, including the schools. One consequence was the emergence of the superintendent as both an educational leader and a business manager, one who tended to see schools as separate from the influences of the larger society. Superintendents, especially in big cities, would fail to see the dissatisfaction with schools that was developing in the 1950s and would intensify in the 1960s and 1970s. Taylor's scientific-management philosophy continued to dominate the preparation and thinking of superintendents, who saw schools as closed systems.

The schools' adaptation of Taylor's factory-style philosophy led to the creation of standards so that the efficiency of schools could be measured. Teachers became workers instead of professionals, pupils were classified and tested in a tightly grade-structured school, extensive records were kept, and standardized tests were given to make sure teachers followed a mandatory curriculum determined by the central office, not by individual schools.

In 1916, Ellwood Cubberly, a professor often credited with shaping the preparation of school administrators, wrote:

> Our schools are, in a sense, factories in which the raw products (children) are to be shaped and fashioned into products to meet the various demands of life. The specifications for manufacturing come from the demands of the twentieth century civilizations, and it is the business of the school to build its pupils to the specifications laid down. This demands good tools, specialized machinery, continuous measure of production to see if it is according to specifications, the elimination of waste in manufacture, and a large variety in the output.[17]

This business orientation, which required an elaborate centralized bureaucracy for the enforcement of standardized educational requirements, made it possible for the superintendent to become the professional expert on what should be taught in schools and how. He (most superintendents were male throughout this period) was viewed as the executive serving a lay board of education. The good-government movement enhanced this change in the superintendent's role.

Members of school boards and city councils ceased being elected by ward and instead stood for at-large elections to smaller bodies; in some cities, school board members were appointed. Elections were moved to off-years from general elections, and party designations were eliminated for school board candidates. This change in school board governance had a profound impact on schools and planted the seeds for conflict seen in some places even today. Frank Lutz and Carol Merz describe the two approaches as "elite" and "arena" boards. Elite boards, they write, "think of themselves as trustees for the people and separate from the people. They usually strive to reach consensus, in private and informal ways, and enact that consensus in the public meeting, by unanimous voice." By contrast, arena boards "think of themselves as 'community *in* council,' that is, they *act* to represent the variety of values and demands inherent in the community as they sit in 'council'... [and] think of themselves as representative *of* the people, dedicated to enacting policy that people demand rather than policy the board, in its wisdom, believes best *for* the people."[18] The elite school board structure and philosophy, along with the ideology of efficiency as the highest priority, dominated urban school systems until the 1960s.

During the early twentieth century, a belief emerged that the schools should be kept out of politics and politics out of the schools. The aim was to take controversial school issues out of the public forum, where they had been under the ward system and arena boards, and make them subject to administrative discretion, the realm of the professional expert. School boards were increasingly populated by businessmen, and this strategy was one with which they were comfortable. But "this was, of course, not de-politicization at all," as historian David Tyack and political scientist Elisabeth Hansot write. "It was another form of politics, one in which authority rested not on representativeness or participation, but on expertise."[19]

The reformers succeeded in buffering the schools from direct political pressure. The superintendent became, in effect, the only important political actor, the only spokesperson for education.[20] He (most were still men) was accepted as the policy advisor to the elite board. Superintendents thought that conflict could be ignored, that differences would disappear. A price would be paid later for this view.

History, however, provides evidence that some big-city superintendents did exercise a political role despite the ideology that schools ought to be apolitical. One of the handful of female urban superintendents during these years was Ella Flagg Young, who served in Chicago from 1909 to 1915. She is described by Tyack and Hansot this way:

> Although she disdained the spoils system and the power of business lobbies in school politics, she was an astute politician in the alternative politics of women's groups and professional associations and a fifty-year survivor in the tumultuous tangle of bureaucratic succession within the Chicago system. Initially trained in the pattern of rigid subordination common to women teachers and eventually presiding over the hierarchy of the second largest bureaucracy in American education, herself compulsively strict in personality, she nonetheless articulated and sought to practice democratic participation in school administration.[21]

13

Further evidence that not all superintendents were politically neutral is found in a description of Frank Cody, Detroit's superintendent from 1918 to 1941. During this period, many superintendents had long tenures, suggesting that they had learned how to work with the politics of their elite boards. Cody certainly had. Appointed in 1918, he lasted on the job 23 years. Tyack and Hansot, together with Robert Lowe, write: "He was an astute politician and publicist who worked effectively with his staff and the elite board.... He urged others to work openly as defenders of the system while he operated behind the scenes with his customary wit and political savvy to influence newspaper people and community influentials."[22] In their 1982 work, Tyack and Hansot make these comments about Cody as well: "Cody never abandoned the political strategies that had linked him successfully to the Detroit community... [He] was a talented politician in both local and national networks and each provided a kind of insurance policy against adversity."[23]

What the boards of the era did not realize, however, was that society was changing. By the 1960s, the conflict they had tried to avoid escalated to the point that schools became almost unmanageable in many cities.

Years of Social Change, 1940–1970

During the Great Depression and through World War II, urban public schools continued down well-worn tracks, preparing the vast majority of children for the factory or domestic pursuits while readying but a small number of middle-class youths for college. The children of wealthy families were educated at private schools. In addition to this social-class division was, of course, racial segregation: white students had their schools and black students their own inferior schools. Boards and superintendents saw their schools as islands removed from the social and political arena around them.

The U.S. Supreme Court's *Brown* v. *Board of Education* decision of 1954, outlawing school segregation, suddenly and deeply stirred up the quiet waters of education. It not only began a painful redrawing of the lines in public schools but helped trigger the civil rights movement and instilled a new racial pride among black Americans. At the same time, the 1950s and 1960s saw the structure of the family changing and the cities losing people and jobs to the booming suburbs. In addition, teachers were being unionized. These many changes had a cumulative impact.

Many superintendents were slow to realize a new day had dawned. They had not been trained to assess outside influences or to plan institutional responses before disruption could become widespread. In 1966 and 1967, three big-city superintendents—Benjamin Willis in Chicago (1953–66), Harold Spears in San Francisco (1955–67), and Carl Hansen in Washington, D.C. (1958–67)—were all dismissed from office because they failed to stay attuned to the social changes that were brewing and disregarded complaints from parent organizations and other community groups. Turmoil in these three school systems brewed for decades.

Role of the Federal Government. During the 1960s, all three branches of the federal government worked to respond to the public's protests and demands for change. The Supreme Court's *Brown* decision , while it was an education case, laid the foundation for barring segregation in all areas of social relations between the races. The decision met with resistance throughout the South for many years; when the lower courts applied *Brown* to *de facto* as well as *de jure* segregation, the decision met similar resistance in the North. For example, in Boston, where *de facto* segregation was ruled unconstitutional in 1974, the school system lost most of its white students and went through a number of superintendents. School leaders were no more prepared to address the dilemmas posed by race than were other leaders.

The courts also began to address the issue of equity in school financing. The root of the school finance issue was, and remains, the wide discrepancy in the amount of money different school districts have at their disposal; this reflects the reliance nearly everywhere on the local property tax. Wealthy suburbs raise far more tax dollars for their schools than do low-income urban and rural areas. Some states go much further than others in trying to make up the difference in property tax revenues. In the early 1970s, cases involving states' responsibility for equitable financing throughout their school districts reached the U.S. Supreme

Court. A number of these early efforts at changing school financing concentrated on poor districts, many of which enrolled a preponderance of minority students.

The first major judicial decision arose from a 1971 case in California, *Serrano* v. *Priest.* The California Supreme Court declared that the state's school finance system violated the equal protection clause of the Constitution: "[T]his is a funding scheme [that] invidiously discriminates against the poor, because it makes the quality of a child's education a function of the wealth of his parents and neighbors."[24]

The school finance issue reached the U.S. Supreme Court in 1973 in *Rodriquez* v. *San Antonio Independent School District.* The justices of the Supreme Court returned the case to the state for resolution, a major setback for those seeking more equitable financing, arguing that "[t]he consideration and initiation of fundamental reforms with respect to state taxation and education are matters reserved for the legislative processes of the various states."[25]

The strategy of using the courts to force school boards and state legislatures to institute more equitable financing of school districts is still being pursued, with a number of cases still pending in state courts.

As states began in the late 1960s to make changes in the methods of funding local schools, superintendents had to become more knowledgeable about state financing—and more political. Acting on President Lyndon Johnson's agenda, both Congress and the executive branch responded to the new demands. The Civil Rights Act of 1964 and the Voting Rights Act of 1965 imposed new mandates on all levels of government to abide by the tenets of equality necessary to a fully democratic society. The enforcement of these laws led to a greater participation of minorities in electoral politics. This, in turn, affected school policies.

More important for education, however, was the Elementary and Secondary Education Act of 1965, which provided large numbers of federal dollars to local schools. While this funding followed the categorical approach (specifying funds for specific purposes), the categories were expanded. "Poor children" or those disadvantaged economically or educationally now became a legitimate category for federal funding. Other titles in the act required a new response from schools—proposals had to be written to gain access to these new federal monies, and if the laws were to be renewed they would have to lobbied for. Finally, along with the funding came regulations, which had to be learned.

The Great Society program included other laws which provided funds to agencies and organizations outside the schools for educational programs. Head Start, the best-known example, was authorized by the Economic Opportunity Act of 1964. School leaders were forced to find out about other social agencies that received these funds and to coordinate their programs with the schools. A more collaborative role for schools was therefore established, though it was accepted only reluctantly by many school leaders, who saw themselves losing their responsibility to provide all the education for all children. Eventually, superintendents and other school leaders learned that their institutions cannot take care of all the problems children bring to school, and today they are more welcoming of collaboration with other agencies and organizations in the community—another example of their changing role.

Congress also passed a new immigration act in 1965 that did away with the quotas favoring immigration from Europe which had existed for most of the century. No one anticipated what this policy change would mean for public schools. The shift in where "new" Americans are coming from has been monumental; immigrants from South and Central America, the Caribbean, and Southeast Asia now constitute the majority of newcomers. The impact has been greatest on schools in New York, California, and Texas. In some New York community school districts, for example, students from these countries already are a majority. School officials have had to respond to the needs and demands of these new populations, another unanticipated change.

The Local Level. In addition to responding to new civil rights mandates and laws at the federal level, in the early 1960s local leaders began to feel new demands and protests close to home. As the civil rights movement grew, schools were boycotted and picketed. In Boston, some independent schools were established by blacks. But these sporadic protests did not bring about the changes in schools that would provide equal opportunity for underserved groups, and African Americans soon saw electoral politics as the next logical step to attaining their ends.

Whites had already begun fleeing the cities during the 1950s, though white enrollment in city schools did not decline precipitously until 20 years later. By the late 1960s, no city or school system yet had a "majority-minority" population (a new label signifying that previously defined minorities were becoming a numerical majority), but this transformation was on the way.

A demand for different leaders was beginning to be voiced. As student enrollment in city schools grew increasingly African American, the desire for superintendents representing this population also grew. The overwhelming majority of the superintendents at this time were white males, and they were criticized as being part of the problem with the schools, especially those in the big cities. These men were not prepared for a shift in roles that would require them to manage conflict and accept protest groups as legitimate voices of the school community. Larry Cuban makes this point, especially about Benjamin Willis in Chicago, in his book *Urban School Chiefs Under Fire*.

One of the superintendents whose long tenure ended just before this period of protest was, surprisingly enough, a woman. Ira Jarrell, who was of course white, oversaw the schools in Atlanta from 1944 to 1960, beginning during the period of legal segregation and staying on until well after the 1954 *Brown* decision. One of Jarrell's top executives was often called the "superintendent for the Negroes." A black superintendent, Alonzo Crim, was appointed in 1972 as a condition of the court order, demonstrating the expanding role of the court in school decisions. Little was done, however, to desegregate the Atlanta schools until extensive court litigation forced action in the 1970s.

Union organizing among teachers and collective bargaining escalated after the 1968 teachers' strike in New York City. The strike was credited with building the United Federation of Teachers in New York City, and chapters of the American Federation of Teachers soon organized in most major cities, replacing the National Education Association as the teachers' collective bargaining unit. The strike in New York City effectively ended an experiment there in community control of the schools, and the residue of that struggle lingers on. Yet the relationship between teachers and the community has reemerged as a factor in the more recent reform movement; witness the new emphasis on school-based management and shared decision-making.

As the 1960s came to an end, the nation—and especially the cities—faced uncertainty. Unrest and demonstrations against the Vietnam War had forced Lyndon Johnson to decline to run for a second term. Richard Nixon was elected in 1968 and reelected in 1972 , by which time the Republican domination of the federal agenda began to be felt. The promises of greater social inclusiveness and a more activist government role in correcting society's inequities, which had started with the election of John F. Kennedy in 1960, seemed to have been abandoned.

In short, the 1960s were a difficult time to be a superintendent. Schools had to cope with more court orders on a range of issues, from desegregation to financial reform to attending to children with special needs and language differences. More state and federal funds were available, but they arrived at the price of more regulations. New groups were demanding a place on school boards and in school leadership positions. Meantime, the nation's school population was declining and rapidly changing from a majority of whites to a numerical majority of minorities. Schools also faced the prospect of reduced resources and an entrenched bureaucracy unprepared for adapting to a new world.

The resulting conflicts, together with superintendents' inability to grasp the political significance of their actions, soon forced many superintendents to resign. As the decade of the 1970s began, there was some hope that a "new breed" of superintendent would be better prepared to cope with the forces buffeting urban schools.

CHAPTER 3

THE ROLE OF THE SCHOOL BOARD TODAY

The school board appoints the superintendent. While public satisfaction with the performance of the superintendent is important to his (or her) continued employment, the views of the school board count most. Lawrence Patrick, former chairperson of the Detroit Public Schools Board of Education, voices the opinion that no matter how popular superintendents may be, they will be retained only if they have the confidence and support of the board members and if those members are reelected.

The school board is a uniquely American institution. To many, it represents the epitome of democracy. A recent study by the Institute for Educational Leadership puts it this way:

> School boards filter, interpret and translate the education goals of the people into a mission for the school district. Ideally, the composition of a board would encompass the spectrum of individual and collective interests within school districts. Obviously, the heterogeneity of most communities makes the achievement of that ideal difficult, if not impossible. Nevertheless, board members are expected to be sensitive to the spectrum of community educational perspectives and expectations. They are also expected to somehow divine community consensus and provide leadership for that consensus.[26]

Local school boards derive their power from the state government, whose constitution charges it with the responsibility of providing education for all of the state's citizens. The states' power to create or eliminate school boards and districts is evident in the figures: The 130,000 school districts in 1920 dropped to barely 15,000 in the early 1990s.[27]

Characteristics of School Boards

A major responsibility of the school board is to appoint the superintendent and set the conditions for employment. This makes it crucial for a candidate for appointment or reappointment to know the characteristics of board members, how they are chosen, when their terms in office expire, and what the current issues before the board are.

The summary description of school boards following is for the 47 largest school systems, members of the Council of Great City Schools as of 1992.

Number of Members. The number of people serving on an urban school board belonging to the Council of the Great City Schools ranges from 5 to 15, but the majority (26 of the 47 member districts) have 7 members. Only one board has 15—Chicago's (see Figure 1; note that in 1995 this number was reduced to 5 by new state legislation, a fact discussed at length below). Most have an uneven number. There does not seem to be any clear correlation between the number of members, their terms of office, and the method by which they are chosen.

Terms of Office. The range for members' terms of office is two to six years. The overwhelming majority have four-year terms—35 of the 47 districts.

More studies are needed about the turnover of school board members; it may be as rapid as that of superintendents. Very often, dissatisfaction may grow over time until it reaches the point of action and an interest group launches a campaign to have its agenda adopted. If elected or appointed, the new group may want to bring in its own superintendent. Turnover was so rapid in the early 1970s that in Washington, D.C., the board that fired Barbara Sizemore in 1975 included only one member who had been on the board that had hired her just two years before.[28] In Detroit, a change in board membership led to the hiring of a new superintendent in 1991. The next election in Detroit saw the defeat of

Figure 1
Characteristics of Big-City* School Boards, 1992

Each pie illustrates how the 47 districts divide by selected characteristics.

Number of Members on Board

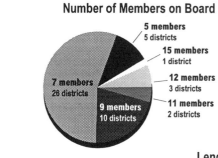

5 members
5 districts

15 members
1 district

12 members
3 districts

11 members
2 districts

9 members
10 districts

7 members
26 districts

Overlap in Terms

Length of Board Members' Terms

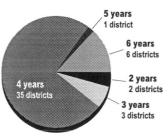

Staggered
39 districts

Concurrent
6 districts

Not reported
2 districts

5 years
1 district

6 years
6 districts

2 years
2 districts

3 years
3 districts

4 years
35 districts

Method of Election/Appointment

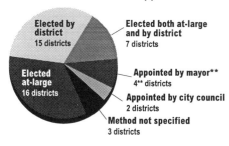

Elected by district
15 districts

Elected both at-large and by district
7 districts

Elected at-large
16 districts

Appointed by mayor**
4** districts

Appointed by city council
2 districts

Method not specified
3 districts

* Defined as the 47 districts belonging to the Council of the Great City Schools.
** One board, New York City's, is "mixed," with two members appointed by the mayor and five by the borough presidents.

23

the superintendent's supporters, prompting her resignation a year before her three-year term expired.

Another example occurred in Boston in 1991, when a new superintendent was appointed by the outgoing 13-member elected board that was to be replaced within a few months by a 7-member board appointed by the mayor. None of the previous committee members was appointed to the new board, so both the structure and members changed.

Boston also illustrates the constraints imposed by two-year terms, especially when all members serve concurrent terms and so come up for election at the same time. On Boston's elected board the members are constantly running for election.

Overlap of Time. Almost all the 47 school systems (39) have staggered terms (only some of the members are elected or appointed any given year), providing for continuity. Only six systems have concurrent terms. The disadvantage of concurrent terms is instability: since all members run at the same time, the majority may be defeated at one fell swoop. If the terms are also short—for example, two years—the entire board may never stop running for reelection.

How Members Are Chosen. The method for selecting school board members is probably the most critical factor in the tenure of a superintendent, requiring him or her to make a careful appraisal of the politics involved in the different systems. Like most school systems in the country, the majority (41 of 47) of the member districts of the Council of the Great City Schools have elected school boards. Sixteen districts elect their members at-large from the whole city or county, 15 elect by specified geographical districts, and 7 use a combination of at-large and district seats (Atlanta, Dade County, Detroit, Indianapolis, Milwaukee, Portland, Seattle and, until 1992, Boston). The remaining 6 school districts have appointed boards. In 4 of these, Baltimore, Boston, Chicago, and Philadelphia, the members are appointed by the mayor. In one, Norfolk, the city council makes the appointments.

Because of its unique governmental structure, New York City has a different system: the mayor appoints two members to a central board, and each of the five borough presidents appoints one for a total of seven.

24

The central board employs a citywide chancellor and is directly responsible for the high schools and some aspects of special education. Other functions, such as staff development, are carried out in cooperation with the districts. New York's system also includes 32 locally elected school boards of nine members each, who serve four-year terms. The local boards are responsible for the elementary and middle/junior high schools and appoint community district superintendents. Each local board is given authority over its budget, which is based on a formula that includes the number of registered students. New York's state legislature appointed a commission in 1991 to examine this system, in operation since 1970, and to recommend changes. As of spring 1995, the commission had not agreed on the changes that would be presented to the state legislature for action.

In 1988, Chicago's system was changed by the Illinois legislature. The only system of its kind, it is has both a 15-member central board and local boards at each school. The members of the central board, nominated from a list prepared by a widely representative advisory group, are appointed by the mayor to serve five-year terms. By state law, each of the 542 schools has its own school board endowed with extensive powers. The composition of the eleven members of each of these local boards is specified by law: six parents, two teachers, two community representatives, and the principal. The members, except for the principal, are elected by their constituencies. These local boards have the power to appoint the principal to a four-year term on a performance contract and they have jurisdiction over curriculum and budget. Some curriculum requirements are also stipulated by law. This system alters the roles played by the citywide general superintendent and the central bureaucracy, as well as the roles played at each local school by the principal, the teachers, and the community.

Since each school in Chicago's arrangement has a mini–school-board, some of the political skills needed by the superintendent must now be learned by the principal. The central bureaucracy, however, has become much more of a service organization, since some control over curriculum and even personnel is now located at the school building. In 1993, Chicago gained a new superintendent, Argie Johnson, who was actively supporting this decentralized system and was developing ways the central office could provide more assistance to local schools, before her departure in 1995.

Unlike many cities, Chicago has several citywide groups—many of them pressured the state legislature to pass the bill creating the current system—that have been monitoring the operation of the local school boards.[29]

Although this change in Chicago has been in effect only since 1988, even more radical changes in governance and the role of the superintendent were enacted in 1995. Responding to many pressures, including pressure from the city's Democratic mayor for more control of the schools, in 1995 the Illinois legislature passed the School Reform Act. This Act gives the mayor of Chicago the power to appoint five people to a Chicago School Reform Board of Trustees and eliminates a slate of board trustees that a grassroots nominating committee had compiled under the previous law. The initial appointed board will serve through 1999, after which time the mayor will appoint a seven-member board to serve four-year overlapping terms.

More significantly for the role of the superintendent, the Act grants the mayor power to appoint administrators, a power until now reserved to the central board of education. To date, Mayor Richard M. Daley has appointed five such administrators: a chief executive officer, who between now and 1999 will assume the powers formerly held by the superintendent, and four other chiefs with responsibility in the areas of education, purchasing, operations, and fiscal matters. Beginning in 1999, a general superintendent will be appointed by the central board.

All five of Daley's new appointees are former employees with his administration, except the chief of education who has had a lifelong career in the Chicago public schools. The chief executive officer appointed by Daley is not an educator but the former budget director. Argie Johnson, who had served only since 1993, was not included in the new administration.

The 1995 Act replaces the subdistricts with six regional offices. It retains the local school boards created by the 1988 legislation, and requires training within six months of members' election. The Act does make it possible for funds to be used differently, and it puts restrictions on the powers of the teachers union.

Characteristics of School Board Members

Nationwide figures for school board members show that a much higher proportion of women are now serving. *Education Vital Signs* has reported that in 1993, 54.7 percent of school board members were male and 39.9 percent were female (5 percent were unidentified). The minority representation, however, is still far from reflective of the country's population: in 1993, 93.8 percent were white, 2.4 percent black, 1.3 percent Hispanic, 0.9 percent Asian, 0.07 percent Native American, and 0.05 percent "Other."[30] The representation on big-city boards of education differs from the national school board averages, showing a much higher percentage of minorities. For example, in 1992 Detroit had eight minorities out of eleven; Cleveland, five of seven; Atlanta, six of nine; and Cincinnati, three of seven. Moreover, appointed boards tend to have a greater variety in representation than elected boards. In 1992, New York's appointed central board had two Hispanics, two blacks, and three whites; Chicago's had seven blacks, four whites, three Hispanics, and one Asian; and Boston's had two blacks, two whites, two Hispanics, and one Asian.

African Americans have managed over time to greatly increase their representation on school boards. In 1970, there were 362 African Americans in elected positions on local school boards, state boards, and institutions of higher education. By 1991 the total had jumped to 1,636.[31] School boards in several cities now have African American majorities; others have a majority-minority when Hispanics are included.

Current School Board Issues

Because big-city school systems receive most of the media's attention, it is easy to forget that in 1989–90 there were more than 15,000 school districts, each containing anywhere from 300 to one million students (see Table 1). (In 1994, the total was less then 14,000 districts.) Half the districts have enrollments of fewer than 1,000; almost three quarters have enrollments of no more than 5,000. Slightly more than half the

Table 1
Public School Districts and Student Population Size: Numbers and Percent
Distribution, 1989–90 School Year

Student Population	Districts		Students
	Number	Percent	Percent
25,000 or more	179	1.1	28.0
5,000 to 24,999	1,392	9.1	33.6
1,000 to 4,999	5,484	35.6	31.2
1 to 999	7,994	51.9	7.3
Zero/not reported	318	2.1	0.0
Totals	**15,367**	**99.8**	**100.1**

Notes: Percentages may not add to 100 because they represent newly combined categories from original source data. Among those districts belonging to the Council of the Great City Schools, all have enrollments of more than 25,000, nine have enrollments of more than 100,000, and four have enrollments of more than 200,000 (New York, Los Angeles, Chicago, and Dade County/Miami).
Source: U.S. Department of Education, National Center for Education Statistics, "Public Elementary and Secondary Schools and Agencies in the United States and Outlying Areas: School Year 1989–90," p. 18.

districts enroll less than 8 percent of all children. The 100 largest school systems represent fewer than 200 districts, yet enroll almost 30 percent of all students and 41 percent of all minority students[32] (see Table A1 in Appendix).

This distribution raises serious questions of equity, equality of resources, and school board representation. Size obviously affects the selection of a superintendent; the demands of a small, homogeneous community are very different from those of a large urban system with a diverse population. Community size may also influence the way educational decisions are made.

The issue that probably has received the most attention over time is the question whether elected boards or appointed boards are the most effective. Good-government groups or those whose priority is broad participation usually favor the elected system. Furthermore, they usually favor district seats rather than at-large seats so that group or neighborhood interests can be represented.

Some favor a combination of at-large and district elections, an approach that Detroit and Atlanta follow and that Boston once followed. There is some evidence that more conflict and disagreement result when the board is combined in this way, however. Boston found that the district members promoted the self-interest of their districts (and sometimes their own interest), often losing sight of the larger concerns of the city. But Detroit did not experience such a conflict. Part of the reason may be that Detroit's board members had arrived at a greater consensus on mission and goals through the way in which they were nominated and elected. This apparent consensus, however, did not guarantee reelection when the reform group lost its majority in the 1993 election.

In New York City, which for years has had a system of combined appointments and elected community boards, the central board has been the scene of many hostile exchanges between members appointed by the mayor and those appointed by borough presidents, as well as conflict between the members and the chancellor. The latter conflict reached its zenith in the early 1990s during the tenure of Chancellor Joseph Fernandez and led to the nonrenewal of his contract for a second three-year term. Ramon Cortines, who followed Fernandez as chancellor, resigned after only two years, not from disagreements with the school board but from disagreements with Mayor Rudolph Giuliani. Several months of intense negotiations resulted finally in a candidate acceptable to Giuliani and the school board: Rudolph Crew, the superintendent (at the time of his selection) in Tacoma, Washington. As of this writing (fall 1995), the New York State Legislature seems ready to seriously address the governance of the system, which has been operating under the 1970 decentralization law that created the complex governance structure for New York City schools described earlier.

Those favoring the appointed system believe that schools should be more closely related to local government, especially in those systems that are fiscally dependent on the mayor or city council for funding. Most favor appointment by the mayor so that accountability for decisions is clear. Critics of appointed boards, however, charge that they are a rubber stamp for the mayor and do not put the welfare of children first, an accusation already made in Boston.

Under the appointment system, the mayor can also influence the selection of the superintendent. In Boston, Mayor Raymond Flynn wanted to delay the appointment of the new superintendent until 1992 when the committee he had appointed would be in power, though the outgoing committee made the appointment anyway. In Baltimore, which also has an appointed board, Mayor Kurt Schmoke influenced the selection of Richard Hunter as superintendent in 1988. In 1991, after it was clear that his three-year contract would not be renewed, Hunter released a statement to the press. Although the mayor and the president of the school board had, according to Hunter's press statement, "enticed me to leave my position as professor at the University of North Carolina at Chapel Hill to come to Baltimore and join their efforts in bringing about a renaissance in public education for the city," Hunter had nevertheless been "set up as a scapegoat to take the blame for this administration's failure to live up to the mayor's campaign promises to the voters of Baltimore."[33]

The turnover of urban superintendents in recent years shows no consistent pattern; superintendents have left or been fired by both types of boards. In Philadelphia, for example, after 10 years in office, Superintendent Constance Clayton had her contract renewed for another four years but then decided to take early retirement in 1993; the membership of Philadelphia's school board, appointed by the mayor, had changed during her tenure. San Diego, whose superintendent Thomas Payzant had also been in office for 10 years, has an elected, at-large board. When Payzant accepted a top position in the U.S. Department of Education in 1993, the board replaced him with the deputy superintendent, Bertha Pendleton, an African American woman who had been in the system for most of her career. In 1995, Payzant was appointed superintendent of schools in Boston, replacing Lois Harrison Jones, an African American woman.

Another criticism of appointed boards is that they are not as representative as elected ones, which allow citizens to choose who will represent them. The evidence does not seem to support this criticism. In Boston and, until recently, Chicago, the mayor has been required to consult a broadly representative advisory group in making board selections. In both cities, as mentioned earlier, the boards are representative of the major racial and ethnic groups. Indeed, the elected, at-large system seems the least likely way for minorities to gain access to boards, since they must appeal to the whole city for votes.

Over the years, some critics have proposed the elimination of school boards altogether in favor of making the schools another city government department like fire, police, or health. Two recent studies of school boards do not propose their elimination but rather recommend ways to strengthen their operation. A 1986 study by the Institute for Educational Leadership found that American society cherishes the school board as an expression of the democratic form of government, despite dissatisfaction with the performance of most boards. According to that study, "The local school board is the only means through which the community expresses itself in respect to education. Boards are the interpreters and translators of need and demand. They mediate between and among conflicting interests. They sort out contending values, and they initiate and enact policies to govern locally."[34] The only alternative might be decision by a bureaucracy, by those who do not have to come in for public scrutiny. Many believe that school boards perform such a necessary function in a diverse community and nation that they must be preserved and strengthened.

The most recent report on school boards, issued in 1992 by the Twentieth Century Fund's Task Force on School Governance, proposes that boards confine themselves to policy making and refrain from collective management. As policy-making bodies, they would be responsible for "setting broad policy guide-lines, establishing oversight procedures, defining standards of accountability, and ensuring adequate planning for future needs."[35] The report adds this suggestion for superintendents: "While professionals would oversee the myriad details of running public schools—as they theoretically do now—they would do so within the constraints and policy parameters established by those governing local education: the education policy boards."[36] The report advises school boards to let the superintendent "manage" the schools.

These reports as well as critics who want to strengthen the role and power of school boards see greater local participation and more representativeness as part of the answer. Certainly the Chicago plan has carried increased participation at the local school level to its logical end. In his study of the origins and first year of the Chicago reform, G. Alfred Hess summarizes the reform's philosophy this way:

> In short, the Chicago reformers felt there were some higher-order values democracy should insist upon, including equality of educational opportunity. Thus, their concern was to find ways to make the system of democratic control work better, rather than to abandon it... Principally, what the Chicago reform approach contends is that what has been lost under large-scale urban bureaucracies is the people's voice... Instead of doing away with democratic control, the Chicago reform effort seeks to put that control in the hands of the *demos*, the people.[37]

CHAPTER 4

MINORITY ISSUES AND URBAN POLITICS

By 1970, social change was sweeping the country at a rapid, almost dizzying pace. No governor, mayor, or school superintendent could afford to ignore the racial, ethnic, and economic transformations sweeping the cities and their public schools. The flight to the suburbs of many middle- and upper-income whites was well under way, causing urban school enrollments to drop and transforming the makeup of the classroom. This trend has still not abated. Studies show that in the northern states, many school systems are even more segregated in 1993 than they had been 20 years earlier.[38] In addition to this racial imbalance, a strong influx of new immigration had begun to intensify both the ethnic diversity and the curricular challenges facing city teachers.

These social trends, coupled with a worsening of urban poverty and an increase in single-parent households, brought severe new strains into the schools, inevitably burdening superintendents with the difficult task of reconciling the demands of several constituencies at once. Because these shifts in the social environment affected schools so immediately and so deeply, they receive a summary review in the next pages. That discussion is followed by a review of the political transformation that naturally occurred in the cities during the period.

As the race and ethnicity of urban populations shifted, so did the race and ethnicity of the cities' mayors and elected school boards, and this in turn meant that for the first time big-city superintendents, usually appointed by the boards, could be persons of color as well. Though Latino populations became quite significant in this regard, particularly in border states and California, by far the most common instances of administrative integration involved black populations electing black mayors and seeing black superintendents appointed.

This chapter therefore pays special attention to the rise of black urban politics during this period. The educational, administrative, and political demands on the superintendent and the racial politics of city and suburb often intersected in the person of the black mayor, who among other challenges had to attract business development, handle controversies over school integration, balance growing costs with declining revenues, and work to keep the school system afloat. The city of Detroit is reviewed as an archetypal case history from which much can be learned.

Demographic Changes

Perhaps the most significant factor for public schools was the changing population of the cities.[39] Here too, superintendents were ill prepared. Some changes could have been predicted, such as changes in birth rates and in ethnic diversity. While these changes may have been irreversible, they could have been responded to with different policies, for example by changing curricula to match the changing backgrounds of the student population. The decline in graduation rates could perhaps have been stemmed by flexible responses of this kind.

During the 1970s and 1980s, total enrollment declined in most of the large cities of the Northeast and Midwest, while it boomed in the cities and suburbs of the South and Far West (the Sun Belt). In some cities, including Cleveland and Atlanta, enrollment fell by half or more in the 20 years from 1967 to 1987. In other cities—Detroit, Chicago, New York, and Philadelphia—it dropped by at least 100,000 (see Table A1 in Appendix).

Accompanying the decline in total enrollment was a change in the composition of the student body, a trend not always reflected in the total city population. The school systems of most big cities are now majority-minority when the numbers of blacks and Hispanics are combined, even though few of the cities (Washington, D.C., and Detroit are two exceptions) show this domination by minority racial groups in their total population.

Desegregation. One reason for this shift both in total enrollment and in the composition of the student body was desegregation. White students began leaving city school systems in large numbers in the mid-1970s, when many big-city school districts were undergoing court-ordered desegregation. Today black and Hispanic students make up a majority in more than half of the nation's largest school systems (see Table A1 in Appendix). A recent study of school desegregation, commissioned by the National School Boards Association and carried out by school integration expert Gary Orfield, indicates the ironic results of white flight: school systems in the North are more segregated today than 20 years ago.[40]

The populations of several large cities, Chicago for example, are only 10 to 20 percent white, making desegregation according to previous plans almost impossible. Philadelphia is under court order to desegregate.[41] The school board is appealing, since 75 percent of the city's 191,000 students are black or Hispanic. Superintendents and school boards must now deal with the desegregation mandates from the courts within the constraints of the students' present racial makeup.

Expanding Immigration. Another reason for the shift in student population was the reform in national immigration policy described earlier. The federal immigration act of 1965 has been amended several times, continuing the policy that opened the doors to immigrants from parts of the world other than Europe. The 1990 census revealed that in the preceding decade the nation had changed more dramatically than at any time in its history, even surpassing the influx of European immigrants at the end of the nineteenth century and the beginning of this one.

Today's immigrants share many of the same aspirations and reasons for coming as did their predecessors, although due to their color, they may experience more discrimination than earlier European immigrants. The debate over how best to teach English as a second language continues, and it has become more complex. Many more languages must be dealt with than ever before and only a limited number of teachers and administrators are prepared to deal with this diversity. One of the major issues concerns how long one should let children learn in their native language with a bilingual teacher before immersing them in English only. The need to learn and understand different cultures has grown apace; yet in many preparation programs for teachers and administrators, neither courses in different cultures nor field, clinical, or intern experiences with diverse populations are required.

Students With Disabilities. The 1970s ushered in another group of students who added to the schools' diverse mix—children with special needs or disabilities. As a result of the Education for All Handicapped Children Act in 1975, subsequent amendments and regulations, and continuing court cases, all school systems are now required to educate all children in the "least restrictive environment." Federal and state directives to implement these new requirements and the continuing demands and concerns of parents and community-based organizations have had a decisive impact on the schools—both in appropriate educational programs for handicapped children and in the reorganization of schools to "mainstream" these children. Superintendents not only had to learn new instructional strategies that needed to be introduced in the classrooms, they also had to hone their negotiating and political skills to deal with the constant pressure from outside groups for change and compliance.

The Changing Family. Far-reaching changes in the family also were underway. The working mother has become a fact of life. Of all children (under age 18), 82 percent now have working mothers, and 60 percent of mothers of preschool-age children (under age 6) work outside the home at least part-time.[42] Other changes in the family also have implications for schools: the number of single-parent families continues to increase; many more families are divorcing; more teenagers are becoming parents; and an alarming number of children are being born addicted to alcohol or drugs, handicapping them from birth. Another phenomenon affecting the schools, especially in big cities, is that of the homeless family. Living on the street or in temporary shelters or hotels, these children are constantly on the move, making it difficult, if not impossible, to educate them.

These changes in family patterns directly affect the schools as well as the children whose families may not be providing the socialization or support needed to do well in school. Educators—administrators, teachers, and support staff—can no longer assume that a child has a nurturing family; the school may have to provide activities, such as recreation and child care, previously undertaken by families, community organizations, or churches. Schools face other challenges as well in response to these changing family circumstances: they must reorient scheduling for parent conferences, locate parent volunteers at a time when so many parents work, and know how to respond legally to the noncustodial parent in a divorced family. Since schools cannot do everything, collaboration with other social agencies is essential.

Many children suffer from poverty. The number has increased to the point that of all Americans in poverty, the largest age-group is children. According to the National Center for Children in Poverty, 17 percent of children below the age of six were living in poverty in 1979, and by 1991 their number had grown to 24 percent (5.6 million children).[43]

Superintendents must reach out beyond the schools to deal with the problems stemming from these changes in families and students. Amid the Great Society programs of the 1960s, far-sighted superintendents and those in institutions of higher education who trained school administrators recognized that schools needed to make alliances and establish collaborations with other agencies and organizations. Schools could not socialize and educate young people by themselves. In many cities, examples now exist of superintendents who exercise political leadership and seek new partnerships with families, social agencies, community organizations, and businesses.

Upon interviewing numerous school principals in New York City, Richard Greenspan, David Seeley, and John Niemeyer found that reaching out to community organizations and social services is important to schools. One New York school, P.S. 218, has an unusual arrangement that offers a model for other cities. The Children's Aid Society, a long-established agency in the city, agreed to locate its facilities in the P.S. 218 building rather than erect a separate facility. This agency has expanded its school presence to include an elementary school, P.S. 5, which was designed and built to accommodate a variety of services. Not only are mental health/social services provided on site, but after-school programs for children and evening classes for parents are as well. The collaboration between this agency and the schools is an excellent example of how educational and social services can work together for children.

Greenspan and his coauthors also describe a statewide effort in Kentucky, which was begun in 1990, to set up a Family Resource Center at or near every elementary school where at least 20 percent of the students were poor, as well as a Youth Service Center at every middle and high school with similar student poverty rates.[44]

There are at least two nationwide efforts to demonstrate how schools and social service agencies can join together to provide a more comprehensive approach to children and families in need of support. The Institute for Responsive Education, located in Boston, has launched several programs to demonstrate how these collaborations can be designed. Its Responsive Schools Project, supported by funds from several foundations, has identified five school districts to develop particular programs to respond to their student populations in a comprehensive, collaborative way.

Another national effort is the work of the National Center for Social Work and Education Collaboration. Under the direction of Fordham University and funded by the DeWitt Wallace–Reader's Digest Fund, this project connects universities and school districts in various parts of the country to jointly prepare teachers and social workers with internships in the same schools. These partnerships can have long-lasting effects on the way children and families are approached in the future.

These examples illustrate the importance to superintendents and principals of knowing what services are provided in the community and developing strategies for building partnerships for the children they serve.

The Advent of Black Mayors

The elections of black mayors, symbols of a change in power, began in Cleveland in 1967 and were followed in Newark (1970), Atlanta (1973), New Orleans (1977), Chicago (1983), Philadelphia (1984), and finally New York (1990). (These first black mayors were not always succeeded by other blacks.)

Has the attainment of political power by black candidates in many cities led to improvements for the black population? As political scientist James Jennings writes, "It is both fact and paradox that at the same time blacks are realizing political gains, social and improved life conditions have generally worsened for this group of American citizens."[45] Aswith the first blacks appointed superintendents of schools, timing may be working against the new political leadership. Two became mayors when the economy was in recession, and all took over when the federal funds so plentiful in the 1960s were being slashed or were disappearing entirely under Republican White House administrations. The movement to the suburbs of middle class residents (black as well as white) and of industrial, business, and other commercial interests was accelerating.

Black mayors, like all mayors, have had to face certain realities. One is that their cities need to provide a healthy environment for business if they are to remain a viable place to live and work in. It has been critical for their administrations to form alliances with busness interests. Second, because of their governmental structure and limited power to raise revenues, by themselves cities are not in a position to solve some of the social problems associated with their increasingly poor populations. Welfare and health programs in particular depend on state and federal funds and, therefore, on political connections. Usually, the people needing these services are among a black mayor's key constituencies. Like their counterparts in the schools, these new black leaders must somehow atisfy the conflicting demands of the predominantly white economic elite, the black middle class, and the black poor.

Changes in City Politics: The Case of Detroit

While many cities and their schools have been losing population, the metropolitan areas surrounding them have been growing. Detroit may be an extreme example of this movement out of the city to the suburbs, including those "outer suburbs" that make up a second, more distant ring around the city and which are becoming more and more self-sufficient.

Not only people have left Detroit. Industrial parks, shopping centers, and cultural institutions have relocated in the suburbs as well, giving suburban residents little need to come to the city. In downtown Detroit there are no longer any major department stores and but a few cultural institutions. Interstate highways provide direct access from the suburbs into the downtown for those who continue to work in the city but do not live there. Both the professional football team, the Lions, and the basketball team, the Pistons, have their stadiums outside the city.

The relocation of businesses means cities lose part of their tax base at the same time tht increasingnumbers of poor residnts need more ciy services, including schools. Wihout greater tax incentives and more generous state and federal funding, the cities are limited in their capacity to reverse the out-migration of citizens and businesses.

An equally significant trend was the advent in the 1970s of what political scientists call "the racial politics of the city." The number of black elected officials has increased tremendously in the past two decades in all parts of the country, with the most significant changes in the South and in large northern cities.

The transformation of city politics followed years in which African Americans concentrated their political energies at the national level. Their tactics, aimed at making their constitutional rights a reality, were litigation in the courts, followed by marches and protests in the street, and finally, participation in the electoral process at both the national and local levels. Since blacks in the 1970s were a minority in nearly all cities, early black candidates for office believed (some still do) that they would be accepted and elected only if they formed coalitions with white interests. Detroit is an example of blacks first using the coalition approach and then, as they became a majority in the city, rallying to elect a candidate who identified himself primarily as a black man.

African Americans have lived in Detroit almost as long as the city has existed. The auto industry and powerful unions provided a stable economy for many years. A black middle class also existed for years, and blacks slowly gained influence in the unions, although a major race riot in 1967 shattered Detroit's image of racial peace.

Detroit's Black Mayors. Blacks in Detroit had long had black political representation in the state legislature (since 1938), Congress (1953), and the city council (1957). But because of the city's strong mayor-council form of government, the election of a black mayor was viewed as the real prize, symbolically as well as actually.

Detroit's first black candidate for mayor, Richard Austin, downplayed his racial identity; he ran in 1969 as a coalition candidate of the establishment. The city was not yet majority black, and Austin failed to win enough white votes to be elected.

By the next election, in 1973, the liberal coalition politics that offered a "safe" black candidate had collided with the movement for black political independence, many of whose tenets had been set forth in the 1967 book *Black Power*, by Charles Hamilton and Stokley Carmichael. The new ideology, reflected in the campaign strategy of black candidate Coleman Young, can be gleaned in the following excerpt from Hamilton and Carmichael's book:

> The concept of Black Power... is a call for black people in this country to unite to recognize their heritage, to build a sense of community. It is a call for black people to begin to define their own goals, to lead their own organizations and to support those organizations. It is a call to reject the racist institutions and values of this society.[46]

Coleman Young had been a labor organizer and state senator, and he gloried in identifying with his black constituency. He was confrontational and did not automatically cater to the white downtown business elite. He also resisted any move toward metropolitan or regional solutions to the city's problems, not wanting to dilute his strong political base in what was now a predominantly black city. Young's election strategy worked because blacks were now a majority and ready for a self-consciously black candidate. He won four straight terms, retiring in 1993.

Young was succeeded by Dennis Archer, a former judge who won not only a majority of black votes but a substantial number of white ones. Some called Archer a coalition candidate, but the term no longer carried the connotation of compromising the needs and concerns of black citizens to win the business elite's support. Like most northern cities but

41

more so, Detroit had been in economic decline for years. Young did not see or did not want to see that without some form of cooperation across the metropolitan area the city would not prosper, but Archer was amenable to seeking such solutions.

At the same time as the community mobilized to elect a black mayor, forces were also seeking the appointment of a black superintendent. A new school governance structure had been adopted in 1971 that combined a central board with regional boards (though this would later be changed to a single citywide elected board). Following the Supreme Court ruling in 1974, Detroit's board appointed its first black superintendent, Arthur Jefferson. Jefferson, who had served in the Detroit system as both a teacher and as a regional superintendent, was supported in the first years of his city superintendency by the board's chairman, a well respected black professor, who died suddenly during his third term. Jefferson was also helped by the U.S. Supreme Court's ruling in *Milliken* v. *Bradley*. He remained inoffice for nearly 15 years, one of the longest tenures of any big-city superintendent, white or black.

School Desegregation. In *Milliken* v. *Bradley*, the first school desegregation case filed against a major northern city, the Supreme Court decision meant that any metropolitan solutions to the problem would have to be voluntary.

The *Milliken* case originated in a suit against Detroit that attempted to show that *de jure* segregation of the schools had taken place even though state law in Michigan did not require it. The federal district court agreed, ruling that *de jure* segregation existed in the Detroit schools due to population shifts, housing patterns, and action by the state and local governments, including school boards. Federal, state, and local government officers and agencies, lending institutions, and real estate firms were all blamed by District Judge Stephen J. Roth for a deliberate policy of segregating housing and thereby the public schools.[47]

Judge Roth further maintained that true relief was impossible within the city limits and that the remedy must include the suburbs. But when the case reached the U.S. Supreme Court, in *Milliken*, the Supreme Court declared that "no remedy was within the equitable power of the District

Court without evidence that the suburban district had committed acts of *de jure* segregation." Integration, at the time defined as some degree of racial mixing of students, was therefore virtually impossible for the Detroit schools, which were already about 70 percent black. The remedy ordered by the Supreme Court did include a range of educational programs for the Detroit schools.

Minorities on School Boards

As minorities became more involved in elections for city offices, they also moved to change the composition of school boards. The elite school boards of the 1930s came under severe attack; in some cities, such as Boston, the legitimacy of the board and the schools themselves was challenged. A change in membership as well as in the system of electoral representation—for example, larger school boards elected from districts—was seen as the first step toward making equity (justice for all elements of the community) a major concern of schooling. The demand for more representation on school boards was, in effect, a call to return to the arena board. Keith Goldhammer describes it this way:

> Heretofore voiceless segments of the community now became vocal and demanded that school officials give attention to the issues that concerned them. The great problem for the school administrator was that he could not remain neutral. Policy that would appease one group would antagonize another... The effective school administrator had to learn how to contain conflict, how to manage conflict, and how to negotiate and win compromises among contending forces.[48]

As school boards became more representative of diverse groups, they were initially somewhat unstable, as evidenced by turnover among members. In the following decades, establishing new working relationships among school board members and superintendents would continue to occupy time and energy.[49]

The Advent of Black Superintendents

Superintendents from minority groups became a possibility as school boards themselves became more representative of minorities. With the student body in city schools growing increasingly African American, the demands grew for superintendents who represented this population and could be role models for it.

It was not until the 1970s that African Americans (most of them men) were appointed to head urban school systems in any number. Considering the thousands of school districts, the 43 black superintendents in the country listed in 1974 nevertheless amounted to a very small number.[50] Even today, the proportion of all school superintendents in the country who belong to any minority group remains disproportionately small. In 1990, 3.4 percent of the nation's approximately 14,000 school districts had minority superintendents (see Tables A2 to A4 in Appendix).

Like the first black big-city mayors, the early black superintendents in large cities were viewed by many constituents as representing their entire race, and extraordinary expectations were placed on them. Yet by the time some were appointed, the problems of urban schools had become so severe that solutions were almost impossible. Many systems had predominantly white school boards that were unwilling to make significant changes in priorities. Black superintendents also faced school bureaucracies that were often unwilling or unable to make the reforms needed. The examples of Barbara Sizemore, the first black woman to become superintendent of a large city (in Washington, D.C., from 1973 to 1975), and Roland Patterson, Baltimore's superintendent from 1971 to 1975, demonstrate how early black superintendents' efforts to make the schools more responsive to the new majority-black student population often were thwarted. Both were dismissed from office.

Barbara Sizemore's superintendency has been described in detail by Nancy Arnez, who based her research on interviews, observations, and an extensive review of documents and newspaper accounts. After examining such external factors as racism, sexism, community pressure groups, and the unique relationship between Congress and the District of Columbia, as well as such internal factors as rapid board changes, role conflict, rules and regulations, and the behavior of the board presidents, Arnez concludes that all these factors "interfered with [Sizemore's] efforts to make the school system more responsive to the needs of the 96 percent black and 70 percent poor population."[51] The conflict mounted until the decision was made to fire the superintendent.

Two other black superintendents appointed in large cities at about the same time did enjoy a long tenure: Arthur Jefferson served in Detroit from 1975 to 1988 and Alonzo Crim, mentioned earlier, in Atlanta from 1973 to 1987.

Some of the early black superintendents were similar to other elected officials in that they came up through the system and did not necessarily see themselves before all else as black. As several said, "I am a superintendent who happens to be black." Some did not try to build a black constituency, wanting instead to be seen as the superintendent of all children, not realizing that these approaches did not have to be mutually exclusive. Some more recently appointed superintendents, however, especially those who head systems that are predominantly African American, have been more outspoken in their efforts to make a real difference in the lives of black students. What makes this strategy risky is the same danger that faces black mayors—much of the power and influence rests with the white establishment; in some cities, this includes a majority of the school board members.

If black students are to become functioning members of the technological society of the next century, superintendents must find ways to change the attitudes and expectations of the teachers, staff, and boards. As activist and educator Ron Edmonds often said, "We know enough to educate all the children; what we need is the will to do so." In the late 1970s Edmonds initiated the Effective Schools Movement, whose hallmark goals included a safe environment for learning, high expectations for children, and systematic assessment of progress.[52]

Like black mayors, black superintendents are symbolic leaders and have an influence beyond their cities. Symbols are especially important to a group long labeled inferior and incapable of carrying out high-level responsibilities. Political scientist Michael Preston and his coauthors make this point about Jesse Jackson's 1984 and 1988 presidential bids: "Symbols influence people's thinking, guide their behavior and shape the political environment. Symbols draw attention and get people to vote their interests. They may help reach people who are typically not motivated."[53] The candidacy of blacks for city offices as well as state and federal positions did attract more blacks to register and vote.

The early black mayors were elected more as "managers rather than tacticians skilled in mass mobilization," according to James Jennings.[54] The same could be said about black superintendents, although those appointed most recently seem more comfortable in the role of political leader, and are more willing to take risks to make the system more responsive, including mobilizing their communities for support.

CHAPTER 5

THE CURRENT REFORM MOVEMENT

The last 10 years have witnessed a procession of calls for reform of the public schools, resulting variously in actual reform plans, the issuance of mandates, the announcement of new goals and standards, or the revision of certification requirements. School curriculum and teacher competency have been most directly cited as targets of criticism, but school boards and superintendents have been implicated (or praised) as essential parts of the system to be changed. Much of the reform has issued at the federal level, which therefore receives special attention in this chapter. At the state level, efforts to change certification requirements and to introduce multicultural elements into the curriculum are two examples of ongoing reform, also discussed here.

The publication in 1983 of *A Nation at Risk* set in motion a movement to reform schools directly. This report was the work of the National Commission on Educational Excellence, appointed by Secretary of Education Terrell Bell during the administration of Ronald Reagan. It maintained that our inability to compete as a nation was due in large part to the poor performance of the schools. *A Nation at Risk* spawned a myriad of reports by almost every group with an interest in or a concern about education—more than 125 national reports through 1993 and many more if individual state reports are included. Largely absent from the debate, however, were superintendents of schools and school boards. Part of the reason was that these reports, prepared primarily by people outside the schools, accused local school leaders and governing boards as being part of the problem.

The series of reports that immediately followed *A Nation at Risk*, widely described as the first wave of reform, called for state departments of education to tighten regulations, increase requirements for graduation, and take other regulatory actions. Before long a second wave had formed; it put more emphasis on improving teacher education and the curriculum. Only one report during this period—published in 1987 by the National Commission on Excellence in Educational Administration— addressed administrators directly. This report did not have many specific recommendations related to the political role of the superintendent, but it did assert that superintendents must be leaders: "They must exercise the wisest kind of political behavior by resolving the conflicting demands of many constituents and, in turn, gain their support for decisions."[55]

School Governance

School boards did not receive direct attention until the publication in 1986 of *School Boards: Strengthening Grass Roots Leadership* by the Institute for Educational Leadership. In 1992, the Institute published a second report, whose objective was "to provide a set of expectations and principles for drastic change in the role and operations of school boards." That same year, the Twentieth Century Fund Task Force on School Governance also published a report with recommendations similar to those made in the Institute's reports.[56]

As a result of the reform movement, states have exercised their regulatory powers, and some have attempted to change their relationship with local school districts. State and local policy mandates are often contradictory, requiring officials at these two levels to work together to resolve differences. Superintendents have no choice but to assume a political role and engage in negotiation and compromise. For example, in 1992, New York Commissioner of Education Thomas Sobol, with the approval of the Board of Regents (the state's governing body for all educational institutions), issued "A New Compact for Learning." This new mandate sets out goals and guidelines for all aspects of educational policies and programs required in local school districts, although the districts have the discretion to implement the goals as they see fit. Reporting procedures and a timetable for action are specified.

48

One item, Regulation 100.11, affects the governance of schools and the role of the superintendent, requiring every school district in New York State to submit a plan for school/site-based management by February 1, 1994, which will require changes not only in the superintendency but also in the position of building principal. An indication of the depth and controversial nature of New York State's 1992 mandate for reform is this requirement that school-based decision-making teams be created, each team including parents (at least one), teachers, and the union representative in the building. These teams are expected to make decisions about curriculum, personnel, and some budget items. Concerns about the role of professional teachers and educators, as opposed to lay citizens, in determining what should be taught and how (within school board policies and state requirements) have already emerged. Political skills—negotiation, consensus building, and compromise—will be needed by principals as well as superintendents to deal with the new building politics. The relationship between the central office and the individual school will also change as more decisions are made at the school. Who will now be accountable for the performance of teachers and students when a team is making many critical decisions?

The number of areas in which states have regulatory powers over public schools signals the importance of superintendents' becoming active in state politics. These areas include planning, curriculum, funding, and the credentialing and licensing of professional personnel. In most states, state funds, which constitute a major portion of a local school district's money, are distributed by state departments of education once they are appropriated by the state legislature on recommendation of the governor.

Certification

In many states, a movement is underway to change the requirements for certifying teachers and administrators. In New York State, for example, the requirements for teachers have already been changed, including the establishment of a test that replaces the National Teacher's Examination. Changes in the credentialing process for administrators were proceeding rapidly as of spring 1994. It is critical that superintendents as well as professors of education administration be part of these discussions. A superintendent must understand the process and know when and how to influence any changes.

Multiculturalism

Another area that has come under intense public scrutiny in recent years is curriculum—specifically, multicultural education—which is also a state responsibility. As enrollment in urban schools has grown more diverse, multicultural education has assumed a new urgency. Defining multicultural education and determinating how to implement it have become highly controversial issues. California and New York State have been in the forefront of the debate, together with the universities and textbook publishers.

Both states have issued new directives to local school boards. California's 1987 mandate, called the History–Social Science Framework ("framework" refers to guidelines or directives), is officially described as "an effort to strengthen education in the history–social science curriculum while building on the best practices contained in previous frameworks."[57] California's framework provides ideas and specific activities for grades kindergarten through twelve. It was developed by a large committee representing all educational constituencies and appointed by then State Superintendent of Public Instruction William Honig. In 1987 it was adopted by the California State Board of Education.

New York State's approach created far more of a controversy than California's. The first report was issued in 1989 by the state-appointed Task Force on Minorities. The opening sentence suggests the tenor of the report:

> African Americans, Asians Americans, Puerto Ricans/Latinos, and Native Americans have all been the victims of an intellectual and educational oppression that has characterized the culture and institutions of the United States and the European American world for centuries.... Task Force members and curriculum consultants found that the current New York State Educational Department curricular materials, though improved

recently, are contributing to the miseducation of all young people through a systematic bias toward European culture and its derivatives.[58]

Because of the allegations and recommendations contained in the Task Force's report, State Education Commissioner Thomas Sobol did not submit it to the regents; instead, he chose one of the established state committees to review the social studies curriculum. The committee concluded its work in 1992 with a report, *One Nation, Many Peoples: A Declaration of Cultural Interdependence,* in which the committee took a more inclusive approach than its predecessor, as the title suggests. It attempted to strike a balance between a more multicultural teaching approach and one that reflects the common heritage of all Americans. This report was adopted by the state's Board of Regents as policy for all school districts.

Because multicultural education deals with values and not merely technical expertise, superintendents are necessarily brought into a political debate. Whose values should be the basis for what is taught? Whose culture? Should the state department of education decide these questions for local districts, or should the local community decide?

The controversy over multicultural education is only the most recent example of the dilemma over values and the schools. As the educational leader in the community, the superintendent has an obligation to take part in the debate. The dilemma is more complicated for African Americans now being appointed to the superintendency, since many people once did not (some still may not) view blacks or women as legitimate candidates for the superintendency itself.

A superintendent must examine her (or his) own values and identity and be willing to make her views known. She must offer leadership even if this means opposing the dominant group in the community or the majority on the school board. Will those in the black community who see a black superintendent more as a symbol of political power than as an educator be willing to hear a voice that speaks to the cultural needs of all the children? How does a black superintendent deal with conflicts in the community over values? Avoiding the issues associated with conflicting values and the community's demand for a voice is no solution, as many superintendents learned in earlier decades.

The Expanding Federal Role

The latest wave of school reform also includes the expanding federal role in local schools. The courts have influenced the direction of school reform by continuing to be involved in school desegregation and equity in financing. More recently, they have ruled on sexual harassment. The courts have also ruled on cases involving students and school personnel and the First Amendment (freedom of expression and religious freedom), the Fourth Amendment (illegal searches), and the Fourteenth Amendment (due process and equal protection of the law).[59] State courts have made rulings on financing school districts, including potentially far-reaching decisions in New Jersey, Texas, and Kentucky.

Congress and the president have continued to play an active role on issues vital to local schools. When Congress passed the Goals 2000/ Educate America Act in April 1994, it was the first time that the states and Congress had united on goals for the nation's schools and offered the schools incentives to pursue them. Although adoption of the goals and standards is voluntary for the states and local school systems, schools that do design programs to achieve the goals will have access to newly available funds. The original six goals were adopted by the states during the administration of President Bush. Congress added two more—one on parent participation and the other on teacher education and professional development. The original six are in these areas: children prepared for school; academic achievement and citizenship; mathematics and science; high school graduation rates; adult literacy and lifelong learning; and safe, disciplined, and alcohol- and drug-free schools.

The Reauthorization of the Elementary and Secondary Education Act, passed by Congress in 1994, will require careful attention by educational leaders to changes that have been made in specific provisions, such as the funding allocation. Federal legislation is especially important to big cities, where the majority-minority population still constitutes the group least well-served by the schools. Federal funds may still constitute only a small percentage of the total monies spent by local schools, but their impact has been great because they are targeted to specific programs and populations.

In 1920, the federal contribution to public schools was only 0.3 percent; the local jurisdictions provided by far the most (83.2 percent), and the states provided the balance (16.5 percent). The federal share increased slowly over the years, reaching the high point in 1980 of 9.8 percent. In that year, the local and state shares were closer to being equal: 43.4 percent local and 46.8 percent state. The figures for 1991 show a drop in the federal contribution to 6.1 percent; the average state share was 47.3 percent and the local share averaged 46.6 percent.[60] These figures represent the average of all states.

With money comes regulation. What has been confusing about federal funding is that each program approved by Congress has had its own set of requirements, regulations, and reporting procedures. Some school districts have established a coordinator of funding sources so that they can complement each other. Since other federal laws fund social services provided by other agencies, it is even more important for school superintendents to reach out to these other agencies and develop new mechanisms for collaboration so that the whole child and total family can be served. The Clinton administration has proposed such collaboration among federal agencies; still needed are similar programs at the state and local levels.

Navigating the School Bureaucracy

The urban school superintendent must also be aware of the internal politics of the bureaucracy. Studying the culture of the system is essential for survival.

Most school systems have continued to follow the scientific management approach, with its hierarchical form of organization, established in the 1930s. But times are changing. The reform movement is moving into another phase, and school restructuring in its many meanings has become the latest clarion call for improving education. This drive to give more discretion to local schools portends role changes for both school principals and district superintendents. None of the experiments—including those in Rochester, New York; Dade County, Florida; and New York City—is old enough to be evaluated. A more radical change in governance has occurred in Chicago: the creation of councils at each city school, endowed with power to appoint the principals and limited discretion over curriculum and budget.

How a superintendent deals with the bureaucracy will depend in part on the culture of the system, the way in which school staff members view the authority built into the superintendency, no matter who fills it, and other factors that may be beyond the superintendent's control. A new superintendent would be prudent to investigate the circumstances under which his or her predecessor left and the image that the staff and community had of the predecessor, since both may influence the reception the new superintendent receives. (A rereading of Machiavelli's *The Prince* might provide clues about strategies to be used.)

Teachers Unions and Collective Bargaining. Collective-bargaining agreements between teachers and urban school systems became widespread in the 1970s and 1980s. Teachers' strikes, once unheard of, are now common in systems large and small. Some have lasted for extended periods, leaving a residue of strong feelings between the staff and administrators. In most states, the local chapters of either the American Federation of Teachers or the National Education Association (now considered a "union" after many years of defining itself as a professional organization) have the legal right to engage in collective bargaining with the school managers. When this collective bargaining began, the model looked to was the industrial union with the employer and employee as adversaries. For some, this model was a radical shift from what they had seen as a collegial, professional relationship between teachers and administrators. Although working conditions for teachers have improved, some believe that this adversarial approach has been detrimental to teachers' professionalism.

Unlike the superintendents, who have been hesitant to see themselves as political figures, teachers' unions, collectively and individually, have not hesitated to become directly involved in partisan politics. In many cities, the union endorses candidates for the school board or may even openly run its own candidates for the board. Unions have also been active at the state and federal level in trying to pass legislation favorable to their causes.

The reform movement of the late 1980s and early 1990s has emphasized restructuring schools, in particular site/school-based management and shared decision making, reforms that change the role of the centralized, district-wide union. Teachers are usually part of the school-based teams, which have the authority to request waivers of union contract provisions in order to carry out the teams' plans for the school. If many waivers are requested and granted, many hard-won gains could be eroded. The principle of local school decision making runs counter to the idea of a district-wide union contract that applies to all teachers and all schools. If waivers are not granted, what impact will this have on the enthusiasm and interest of those (including the teachers who want to respond to local needs) trying to develop alternative programs? Community representatives and parents are on many of these teams. What will be their reaction to teachers who may appear more concerned with keeping the contract intact than with doing what is best to educate the children in their charge? This dilemma is just beginning to surface, but as mentioned earlier, avoiding conflict is no solution. The superintendent may have to find ways to deal with this issue.

A question often asked is this: What should be the role of the superintendent in collective-bargaining sessions? Robert Peterkin, former superintendent in Cambridge, Massachusetts, and Milwaukee, Wisconsin, believes that the superintendent should not be an active participant though he or she must be kept informed at all times. By staying out of the ongoing sessions, the superintendent can step in if an impasse occurs and offer suggestions for resolution. Similarly, Floretta McKenzie, former superintendent in Washington, D.C., maintains that by staying out of the actual negotiations, the superintendent is more likely to be seen as an education statesman whose major concern is children's welfare. Both Peterkin and McKenzie stress the need for the superintendent to employ someone highly skilled in negotiating. They also agree that school board members should not be direct participants but must be kept well informed during the talks so that the final agreement contains no surprises.

Community Partnerships

Schools have always recognized that the involvement of parents in schools can be beneficial. Too often, school officials define the parameters of the roles, but this too is changing, as more and more evidence shows that partnerships with families and communities, not mere involvement, can make a difference not only in student achievement but in support for schools. Parents can be the best advocates for school programs. Where school boards are elected, families can become a potent political force. It behooves the superintendent to learn about various types of parent participation that have proved effective in promoting school programs and to help principals develop partnerships at the school level.

Businesses are yet another potential partner with schools, whether contributing computers or other new technology, providing volunteers who work directly with students, or offering more extensive assistance. In New York City, one businessman has persuaded major companies (e.g., MasterCard) located near a public school to extend their lunch hours so employees can spend the time reading and talking with students. Some 200 volunteers are now involved. In both Detroit and Boston, the chambers of commerce and other businesses provide college scholarships for students who do well. To develop these partnerships, the superintendent and the school principals need to arrange for a staff person to work out the details after they have contacted business leaders. Teachers can also be directly involved through "internships" in businesses during the summer or by taking students on field trips to workplaces to expose them to new fields and occupations.

CHAPTER 6

SUMMARY AND IMPLICATIONS FOR THE FUTURE

The public school superintendent has evolved over nearly two centuries from a clerk for the local schools to the most prominent educational leader in the community. The superintendent is perceived as the guardian of a sacred trust—the community's children—and protector and promotor of a revered value: the education of the next generation. The community expects the superintendent to provide the vision, the mission that will guide the schools in preparing that generation.

To fulfill this daunting role, superintendents must be both executives and educational leaders. Both roles have a political dimension, which calls for the ability to work with an array of conflicting interests and forces to maintain a school system able to accomplish its many goals. Superintendents must maintain the stability of the system while adapting to a turbulent environment.

Since the 1970s, external and internal forces have converged in such a way as to make the job of the superintendent more complicated. The ideology that worked to separate schools from politics has led, ironically, to consequences that have made it difficult for schools to adapt to changing conditions in society. Urban school superintendents must learn from the past and understand politics at all levels, since it is only by becoming more politically aware and astute that they will be able to guide educational institutions.

The major changes in the external environment that accelerated in the 1970s have grown even stronger in the early 1990s. The first change is a decline in school population, especially in certain cities. At the same time, the student population has changed from a white majority to a majority-minority in almost all urban school systems. Changes in immigration laws have contributed to this diversity, so that city schools have increasing numbers not only of African Americans but of students from South and Central America and the Caribbean, from a variety of Asian countries, including Korea, Vietnam, Cambodia, the Philippines, Japan, and China, and from Eastern and Western Europe, including Russia. Integration based on a racial balance of blacks and whites is no longer a sufficient goal for urban schools. Multicultural education has become a necessity.

Family patterns are changing as well. "Traditional" families (the father working outside the home and the mother staying at home) with children under age six now make up just 27 percent of all families, down from 47 percent in 1976.[61] Single-parent families, step families, foster and adoptive families, and teenage parents are part of these new patterns. Closely related to these changes is the increasing number of families with small children in poverty. The school population also includes many more children with special needs due to handicaps. Schools cannot reverse these trends, but they can revise their programs to better serve the changing populations.

As a result of federal legislation, funds, though decreasing in the 1980s, are available to schools for targeted programs. But with the money comes more mandates and regulations. The states have also increased their control over curriculum, graduation requirements, the licensing of teachers, planning, and evaluation. Finally, the courts have been more involved in directing what schools can and cannot do, not only in desegregation cases but in school financing and special education. Clearly, schools are in the political arena.

Another influence on urban schools has been the growing ranks of black elected officials. Some cities now have or have had black mayors, a symbol to the community that political control has passed to a new breed of leaders. Unfortunately, many cities are experiencing economic decline and deteriorating neighborhoods. Since the white business elite holds most of the economic power of the cities, the priority for revitalizing most cities has been to redevelop downtown areas. At the same time, city residents have migrated to the inner and outer ring suburbs in increasing numbers. Business and commercial interests have followed the migrating residents or even preceded them, so that these suburbs are becoming self-sufficient. In the meantime, the suburban schools have maintained their separate jurisdictions. The U.S. Supreme Court's 1974 *Milliken* ruling, which denied a mandatory metropolitan solution to the segregation of Detroit's schools, provided the legal basis for suburbs to keep their own schools. Some districts (Boston, Milwaukee, St. Louis, and Hartford among others) have tried voluntary arrangements to integrate city and suburban schools, but the results have been mixed, depending on the criteria used to measure success.

Internally, schools have changed as teachers' unions have grown in size and power, and more recently with the reform movement's recommendation that more control be placed at the local school level through school-based management and shared decision making. These newer reforms may affect union contracts. Parental involvement in the schools marks another effort to improve schools.

Since the 1970s, more African Americans (including a few women), and recently more Hispanics as well, have been appointed to the superintendency. As with the election of black mayors, these individuals are viewed as symbols of change. Their prominence has gone beyond their own community; they are regarded as representatives of their group. A dilemma faces these black leaders: they must be superintendents of all the people and at the same time meet their black constituents' expectation that black children will be given a better opportunity for success.

In light of the impact of these social changes on the public schools, the urban superintendent needs to look at what led to the ideology that schools should be separated from politics and see if the argument is still valid. Although such a separation in fact was not always realized, the belief in it has persisted. It is understandable that a school administrator might want to shun the label "politician," especially at the turn of the century when the superintendency was just being established, for prestige has not always been granted to the politician in our society. Rewards and benefits in America have tended to go to wealthy people or professionals—people who are assumed to hold high principles or at least to be above the political fray. In addition, a tradition of the dedicated civil servant has been lacking in America; here the bureaucrat or career officer has more often been characterized as being without enterprise or imagination. Given a choice between bureaucrat and political opportunist, it is not surprising that the early educational administrators chose neither but looked to the professional as a model.

At the local level, it was hoped that the school board would attract civic-minded people. But even with the coming of at-large, nonpartisan elections that emerged from the good-government movement, it was not possible to eliminate the bargaining, compromising, and promising of favors characteristic of any campaign for public office. These activities, seen by many as the rules of the political game, have continued apart from partisan politics in more factional and confrontational ways. Nevertheless, some separation from politics did take place. This too has had its drawbacks. By separating education from the political conflicts waged over other public services, a narrow base of concern for education was created rather than a community-wide commitment. The belief spread that schools were primarily the concern of those who used them—that is, parents and children. Superintendents now must convince the rest of the community that the schools belong to them too.

For their own part, many superintendents have failed to see that the problems manifest in the schools were interrelated with broader community problems. Too often, they have been totally unaware of other services available to address such problems and therefore unaware of ways those services could be improved or used in collaboration with the schools. Recent cuts in school budgets have made it essential that superintendents today learn of services that can be supplied by community agencies, rather than expecting schools to do everything.

Some school districts are fiscally independent, able to raise their own funds and allocate them directly to the schools. This arrangement does provide some guarantee of continuity, but it can also be inflexible and it may mean going to the voters for budget approval. The experience of many states is not encouraging; school budgets have failed many times. Funding through the general government also has drawbacks, but at least the forum for negotiation is there and supporters can be rallied to help the schools.

Although the revenue for most school districts comes from state and local sources, the federal government continues to have an influence because of its targeted approach, by which funds are set aside to pursue national priorities such as teaching science and foreign languages, giving schools incentives to adopt new programs. The major pool of federal funds continues to be the Elementary and Secondary Education Act, originally passed in 1965 and reauthorized with some significant changes in 1994 for five years under the title, Improving America's Schools Act. In addition, the federal government allocates funds for educational programs to agencies outside the schools. For example, the Economic Opportunity Act of 1964 included funding for Head Start. With the recent emphasis on integrated services and collaborative efforts to bring schools and social service agencies together, superintendents need to be aware of these possibilities so they can take advantage of new sources of funds. Funds for educational purposes may also be available for community development or community-based organizations. Superintendents need to be aware of how partnerships with these groups can be formed, emphasizing again the need to know the community.

School administrators schooled in the avoidance of politics have tended to shun conflict and controversy. They have been ill prepared to participate in public policy decision making, including the recent reforms introduced at both the state and federal levels. The superintendents of the 1950s and 1960s were overwhelmed by the attacks of civil rights groups and caught unaware when the bases of power shifted both locally and nationally. While the new breed of superintendents seem to have learned this lesson, their preparation programs still may not sufficiently emphasize this aspect of the job.

Implications for the Future

Where does the urban superintendent go from here? The first step is a reorientation to the community and a new conception of community. School administrators must no longer look only to the town or city where they are employed. Their perspective should be broadened in recognition of the fact that our society is part of an ever-widening, growing network of interdependence that binds all of us and our activities into one system. They should recognize that what happens at the state, national, and even international level can affect the local school system. They are likely to look for ways to have a voice in determining public policy at every level.

A second aspect of reorientation to the community will be a heightened awareness and deeper knowledge of the programs and services of other agencies in the same community. It may be to the schools' advantage for other agencies to sponsor certain programs, particularly in areas of the cities where confidence in the school system has been replaced by hostility and mistrust but where community-based agencies are still seen as helpful.

A third aspect of reorientation to the community concerns power and influence. Superintendents need to know how to analyze the power structure and learn to know who the influential players are. This includes knowing the interest groups in the community and how their agendas can be meshed with those of the schools.

As superintendents become more skilled in defining the community, their energies will be directed at managing conflict rather than eliminating it. Superintendents will, however, continue to face a dilemma. As Arthur Blumberg writes:

> In order to maintain the system so that the school board is pleased with its peacefulness, conflict must be anticipated, confronted, and diminished. However, in addition to reacting to potential or actual conflict and dealing with it in his organizational maintenance role, the superintendent who would lead must seek conflict out and occasionally promote it.[62]

To know when to provoke conflict, superintendents must weigh the risk of achieving their immediate goal at the cost of losing political capital with school boards or other constituencies or even of losing their jobs. In addition, superintendents must assess a divided community, both critics and supporters. It behooves superintendents to work on building community support for programs.

A New Relationship With the School Board. The controversy over the relative effectiveness of elected versus appointed school boards continues, as does the question whether appointed boards will be as representative as elected ones. New governance structures are being tried. The most radical experiment is Chicago's, described earlier, where a separate school board has been established for every school. Boston now has a school committee appointed by the mayor after more than a century with an elected board. The relationship between school board and superintendent demands constant attention and communication.

Politically attuned superintendents will be able to see their relationship with the school board—their key political connection—in a new light. They can continue in their role as educational leaders and policy advisors to the lay boards that represent the public. But superintendents must also be mindful of the political ramifications of policy decisions, working for constant, open, and honest communication with their boards and pointing out the political implications of board actions. In our cities today, where race continues to be a dominant issue, the superintendent—white, black, or Hispanic; male or female—will have to work to resolve conflicts that are certain to arise. At the same time, any superintendent representing a particular constituency will have to remain aware of his or her obligations to meet that constituency's special expectations.For her or his own survival, there is certain information about school board members that a superintendent needs to know: most importantly, how members are chosen. If the board is elected, the superintendent must be aware of how candidates for the board—the superintendent's supporters and detractors—conduct their campaigns, which interest groups support various members, and what the views of the media are. It may be difficult, however, for a superintendent to decide how direct a role she should play in the actual election. It can be dangerous to support one candidate or slate so publicly that if the candidate or slate is defeated the superintendent can be assured of making enemies. Still, a superintendent must have confidantes who can assess the power of the various candidates and their supporters to gain a sense of what the new board will be like.

If the board is appointed, however, the superintendent needs to assess those who do the appointing. It may be critical before accepting the superintendency to find out the terms of those who make the appointments. There are many cases in which those who make the appointments leave office and the board changes before the superintendent's term ends. Detroit and New York City are recent examples of a change in board composition that led to the superintendent's departure.

Another factor to be investigated is the racial and gender makeup of the board, for these characteristics may influence the priorities and perspectives of various board members. Skills in group dynamics and team building are essential to a superintendent, especially with a diverse board. The superintendent must decide whether some "social distance" is needed, especially if the superintendent is a woman. Finally, any superintendent must be prepared for the unexpected and for board members to change their views as well as their relationship with him or her.

The future is not certain. The task of preparing young people for the next century is overwhelming. The need has never been greater or more urgent for superintendents who can envision the future and give schools the mission of offering what is needed for the next generation. Yet people willing and able to assume these awesome tasks are available. Let us hope school boards choose leaders from among these people and hope as well that the leaders they choose are politically attuned.

NOTES

1. National Education Association, Educational Policies Commission, *The Unique Role of the Superintendent of Schools*, 1.

2. Arthur Blumberg, *The School Superintendent*, 30.

3. Blumberg, *The School Superintendent*.

4. Blumberg, *The School Superintendent*.

5. L. Harmon Zeigler, Ellen Nehoe, and Jane Reisman, *City Managers and School Superintendents' Response to Community Conflict*, 1.

6. L. Harmon Zeigler, M. Kent Jennings, and G. Wayne Peak, *Governing American Schools*, 6.

7. Stephen Bailey, Richard Frost, Paul Marsh, and Robert Wood, *Schoolmen and Politics*, vii.

8. Robert Crowson, *School-Community Relations Under Reform*, 85.

9. Crowson, *School-Community Relations Under Reform*, 96.

10. Blumberg, *The School Superintendent*.

11. Zeigler, Nehoe, and Reisman, *City Managers and School Superintendents' Response to Community Conflict*, 71.

12. Frank Lutz and Carol Merz, *The Politics of School-Community Relations*, 154.

13. Zeigler, Nehoe, and Reisman, *City Managers and School Superintendents' Response to Community Conflict*, 10.

14. Zeigler, Nehoe, and Reisman, *City Managers and School Superintendents' Response to Community Conflict*, 10.

15. Lawrence Cremin, *American Education: The Metropolitan Experience;* Larry Cuban, *Urban School Chiefs Under Fire;* Diane Ravitch, *The Great School Wars* and *The Troubled Crusade: American Education 1945-1980;* Joel Spring, *American Education;* David Tyack, *The One Best System: A History of American Urban Education;* David Tyack and Elisabeth Hansot, *Managers of Virtue: Public School Leadership in America 1820-1980;* David Tyack, Robert Lowe, and Elisabeth Hansot, *Public Schools in Hard Times: The Great Depression and Recent Years.*

16. As quoted in Larry Cuban, *Urban School Chiefs Under Fire*, 119.

17. As quoted in Raymond Callahan, *Education and the Cult of Efficiency*, 152.

18. Lutz and Merz, *The Politics of School-Community Relations*, 57.

19. Tyack and Hansot, *Managers of Virtue*, 108.

20. Donald Mitchell, "Education Politics for the New Century: Past Issues and Future Directions."

21. Tyack and Hansot, *Managers of Virtue*, 194.

22. Tyack, Lowe, and Hansot, *Public Schools in Hard Times*, 91.

23. Tyack and Hansot, *Managers of Virtue*, 146.

24. As quoted in Spring, *American Education*, 287.

25. As quoted in Spring, *American Education*, 287.

26. Institute for Educational Leadership, *School Boards: Strengthening Grass Roots Leadership*, 14.

27. The Twentieth Century Fund Task Force on School Governance, *Facing the Challenge*, 54.

28. Nancy Arnez, *The Besieged School Superintendent: A Case Study of School Superintendent–School Board Relations in Washington, D.C., 1973-1975.*

29. G. Alfred Hess, *School Restructuring, Chicago Style.*

30. *Education Vital Signs, The Executive Educator*, December 1993, A16.

31. Joint Center for Political and Economic Studies, *Black Elected Officials: A National Roster*, 1970 and 1992 editions.

32. U.S. Department of Education, National Center for Education Statistics, "Public Elementary and Secondary Schools and Agencies in the United States and Outlying Areas: School Year 1989–90—April 1991 Final Tabulations."

33. *The Baltimore Afro American*, August 3, 1991, A7.

34. Institute for Educational Leadership, *School Boards*, 14.

35. Twentieth Century Fund Task Force on School Governance, *Facing the Challenge*, 5.

36. Twentieth Century Fund Task Force on School Governance, *Facing the Challenge*, 5.

37. Hess, *School Restructuring, Chicago Style*, 204–205. Hess is executive director of the Chicago Panel on Public School Policy and Finance, a multiracial, multiethnic coalition of 20 nonprofit agencies dedicated to improving public education in Chicago.

38. Gary Orfield, *The Growth of Segregation in American Schools: Changing Patterns of Separation and Poverty Since 1968.*

39. In his 1992 report of current population trends in the United States and projections for the future, Harold Hodgkinson details the changes by region and by state, including the composition of student enrollment, high school graduation rates, racial differences, and additional valuable information for planning.

40. Orfield, *The Growth of Segregation in American Schools.*

41. *New York Times*, February 5, 1994.

42. Harold Hodgkinson, *All One System: Demographics of Education, Kindergarten Through Graduate School*, 4.

43. National Center for Children in Poverty, "Five Million Children: A 1993 Update."

44. Richard Greenspan, David S. Seeley, and John H. Niemeyer, *The Vital Importance of Mental Health/Social Services in School Reform.*

45. James Jennings, *The Politics of Black Empowerment: The Transformation of Black Activism in Urban America*, 109.

46. Charles V. Hamilton and Stokely Carmichael, *Black Power: The Politics of Liberation in America*, 44.

47. Joe T. Darden, Richard C. Hill, June Thomas, and Richard Thomas, *Detroit: Race and Uneven Development*.

48. Keith Goldhammer, "Roles of the American School Superintendent, 1954–1974," 155.

49. See case studies of Atlanta, Detroit and Milwaukee in Barbara L. Jackson and James Cibulka, "Leadership Turnover and Business Mobilization: The Changing Political Ecology of Urban School Systems."

50. Hugh Scott, *The Black Superintendent: Messiah or Scapegoat?*, 43.

51. Nancy Arnez, *The Besieged School Superintendent*, xii.

52. Ron Edmonds, "Effective Schools for the Urban Poor"; "Making Public Schools Effective"; "Programs of School Improvement: An Overview."

53. Michael B. Preston, Lenneal J. Henderson, and Paul L. Puryear, *The New Black Politics: The Search for Political Power*, 32.

54. Jennings, *The Politics of Black Empowerment*, 116.

55. The National Commission on Excellence in Educational Administration, *Leaders for America's Schools*, 7.

56. Institute for Educational Leadership, *Governing Public Schools: New Times, New Requirements*; and The Twentieth Century Fund Task Force on School Governance, *Facing the Challenge*.

57. California Department of Education, *History–Social Science Framework for California Public Schools, Kindergarten Through Grade Twelve*.

58. New York State Department of Education, Task Force on Minorities, *Curriculum of Inclusion*, iii.

59. Crowson, *School-Community Relations Under Reform*.

60. The Council of the Great City Schools, *The Conditions of Education in the Great City Schools*, 398.

61. Committee for Economic Development, Research and Policy Committee, "Why Child Care Matters," 5.

62. Blumberg, *The School Superintendent*, 208. Hall, Beverly. 1990. *Leadership: The Black Urban Superintendency and School Reform in New York City*." Doctoral dissertation, Fordham University, Graduate School of Education.

BIBLIOGRAPHY

American Association of School Administrators, Office of Minority Affairs. 1983. *Perspectives on Racial Minority and Women School Administrators.* Arlington, Va.

——. 1985. *Women and Minorities in School Administration.* Arlington, Va.

——. 1990. *Women and Minorities in School Administration: Facts and Figures 1989–90.* Arlington Va.

Arnez, Nancy. 1981. *The Besieged School Superintendent: A Case Study of School Superintendent—School Board Relations in Washington, D.C., 1973–5.* Washington D.C.: University Press of America.

Bacharach, Samuel, ed. 1990. *Education Reform: Making Sense of It All.* Boston: Allyn and Bacon.

Bailey, Stephen, Richard Frost, Paul Marsh, and Robert Wood. 1962. *Schoolmen and Politics.* New York: Syracuse University Press.

Blumberg, Arthur. 1985. *The School Superintendent: Living With Conflict.* New York: Teachers College Press.

Boyd, William, and Robert Crowson. 1981. "The Changing Conception and Practice of Public School Administration." In *Review of Research in Education*, vol. 9, edited by David Berliner. Washington, D.C.: American Educational Research Association.

Browning, Rufus P., Dale R. Marshall, and David H. Tabb. 1984. *Protest Is Not Enough: The Struggle of Blacks and Hispanics for Equality in Urban Politics.* Berkeley: University of California Press.

——. 1990. *Racial Politics in American Cities.* New York: Longman.

California Department of Education. 1987. "History-Social Science Framework for California Public Schools—Kindergarten through Grade Twelve." Sacramento, Calif.

Callahan, Raymond. 1962. *Education and the Cult of Efficiency.* Chicago: University of Chicago Press.

Catalyst: Voices of Chicago School Reform. 1995. September.

Committee for Economic Development, Research and Policy Committee. 1993. *Why Child Care Matters: Preparing Children for a More Productive America.* New York.

The Council of the Great City Schools. 1990. *The Conditions of Education in the Great City Schools: A Statistical Profile, 1980–86.* Washington D.C.

Cremin, Lawrence. 1988. *American Education: The Metropolitan Experience.* New York: Harper & Row.

Crowson, Robert. 1992. *School–Community Relations Under Reform.* Berkeley: McCutchan Publishing Corp.

Crowson, Robert, and William Boyd. 1992. "Urban Schools as Organizations: Political Perspectives." In *The Politics of Urban Education in the United States* (The 1991 Yearbook of the Politics of Education Association), edited by James Cibulka, Rodney Reed, and Kenneth Wong. London: The Falmer Press.

Cuban, Larry. 1976. *Urban School Chiefs Under Fire*. Chicago: University of Chicago Press.

Cunningham, Luvern, Walter Hack, and Raphael Nystrand, eds. 1977. *Educational Administration: The Developing Decades*. Berkeley: McCutchan Publishing Corp.

Cunningham, Luvern, and Joseph Hentges, eds. 1982. *The American School Superintendency*. Arlington, Va.: American Association of School Administrators.

Darden, Joe T., Richard C. Hill, June Thomas, and Richard Thomas. 1987. *Detroit: Race and Uneven Development*. Philadelphia: Temple University Press.

Edmonds, Ron. 1979. "Effective Schools for the Urban Poor." *Educational Leadership*, No. 37.

————. 1981. "Making Public Schools Effective." *Social Policy*, No. 12.

————. 1982. "Programs of School Improvement: An Overview." *Educational Leadership*, No. 40.

Educational Vital Signs, Executive Educator. 1993. December.

First, Patricia F. , and Herbert Walberg, eds. 1992. *School Boards: Changing Local Control*. Berkeley: McCutchan Publishing Corp.

Fuhrman, Susan H. 1989. "State Politics and Education Reform." In *The Politics of Reforming School Administration* (The 1988 Yearbook of the Politics of Education Association), edited by Jane Hannaway and Robert Crowson. London: The Falmer Press.

Glass, Thomas E., ed. 1992. *The Study of the American School Superintendency, '92: America's Leaders in a Time of Reform*. Arlington, Va.: American Association of School Administrators.

Goldhammer, Keith. 1977. "Roles of the American School Superintendent, 1954-1974." In *Educational Administration: The Developing Decades*, edited by Luvern Cunningham, Walter Hack, and Raphael Nystrand. Berkeley: McCutchan Publishing Corp.

Greenspan, Richard, David S. Seeley, and John H. Niemeyer. 1993. "The Vital Importance of Mental Health/Social Services in School Reform." Report no. 3 in the series, *Principals Speak*. New York: The Research Foundation of The City University of New York.

Hamilton, Charles V., and Stokely Carmichael. 1967. *Black Power: The Politics of Liberation in America*. New York: Random House.

Hess, G. Alfred. 1991. *School Restructuring, Chicago Style*. Newbury Park, Calif.: Corwin Press.

Hodgkinson, Harold. 1985. *All One System: Demographics of Education, Kindergarten Through Graduate School.* Washington, D.C.: Institute for Educational Leadership.

———. 1992. *A Demographic Look at Tomorrow.* Washington, D.C.: Institute for Educational Leadership.

Institute for Educational Leadership. 1986. *School Boards: Strengthening Grass Roots Leadership.* Washington, D.C.

———. 1992. *Governing Public Schools: New Times, New Requirements.* Washington, D.C.

Jackson, Barbara L. 1967. "The Role of the Superintendent as a Politician." Unpublished manuscript. Harvard Graduate School of Education.

———. 1989. "Race, Ethnicity, Culture, and Values: A New Emphasis Needed in Administrator Preparation Programs." *Improving the Preparation of School Administrators, Notes on Reform,* No. 6. Charlottesville, VA: The National Policy Board for Educational Administration.

Jackson, Barbara L., and James Cibulka. 1992. "Leadership Turnover and Business Mobilization: The Changing Political Ecology of Urban School Systems." In *The Politics of Urban Education in the United States* (The 1991 Yearbook of the Politics of Education Association), edited by James Cibulka, Rodney Reed and Kenneth Wong. London: The Falmer Press.

Jennings, James. 1992. *The Politics of Black Empowerment: The Transformation of Black Activism in Urban America.* Detroit: Wayne State University Press.

Joint Center for Political and Economic Studies. 1970. *Black Elected Officials: A National Roster, 1970.* Washington D.C.

———. 1993. *Black Elected Officials: A National Roster, 1992–93.* Washington, D.C.

Knezevich, Stephen J., ed. 1971. *The American School Superintendent.* Arlington, Va.: American Association of School Administrators.

Lutz, Frank, and Carol Merz. 1992. *The Politics of School–Community Relations.* New York: Teachers College Press.

Mitchell, Donald. 1989. "Alternative Approaches to Labor-Management Relations for Public School Teachers and Administrators." In *The Politics of Reforming School Administration* (The 1988 Yearbook of the Politics of Education Association), edited by Jane Hannaway and Robert Crowson. London: The Falmer Press.

———. 1990. "Education Politics for the New Century: Past Issues and Future Directions." *In Education Politics for the New Century* (The 1989 Yearbook of the Politics of Education Association), edited by Donald E. Mitchell and Margaret E. Goertz. London: The Falmer Press.

Moody, Charles. 1983. "On Becoming a Superintendent: Contest or Sponsored Mobility?" *The Journal of Negro Education,* vol. 52(4): 383-97.

National Alliance of Black School Educators. 1992. *Superintendents' Commission Directory.* New York: New York University.

National Center for Children in Poverty. "Five Million Children: A 1993 Update." New York.

National Center for Social Work and Education Collaboration. 1995. *Conversations* (newsletter). February issue.

The National Commission on Excellence in Educational Administration. 1987. *Leaders for America's Schools.* Tempe, Ariz.: University Council for Educational Administration.

National Education Association, Educational Policies Commission. 1965. *The Unique Role of the Superintendent of Schools.* Washington, D.C.

National School Boards Association. 1992. *Urban Dynamics: Lessons in Leadership from Urban School Boards and Superintendents.* Alexandria, Va.

New York State Education Department. 1991. *A New Compact for Learning: Improving Public Elementary, Middle, and Secondary Education Results in the 1990s.* Albany, N.Y.

New York State Education Department, Social Studies Review and Development Committee. 1991. *One Nation, Many Peoples: A Declaration of Cultural Interdependence.* Albany, N.Y.

New York State Education Department, Task Force on Minorities: Equity and Excellence. 1989. *Curriculum of Inclusion.* Albany, N.Y.

Orfield, Gary. 1983. *Public School Desegregation, 1968–1980.* Washington, D.C.: Joint Center for Political Studies.

———. 1993. *The Growth of Segregation in American Schools: Changing Patterns of Separation and Poverty Since 1968.* A report of the Harvard Project on School Segregation to the National School Boards Association. Alexandria, Va.: National School Boards Association.

Orfield, Gary, and Franklin Monfort. 1988. *Racial Change and Desegregation in Large School Districts: Trends Through 1986–87 School Year.* A report to the National School Boards Association Council of Urban Boards of Education. Alexandria, Va.: National School Boards Association.

———. 1992. *The Status of School Desegregation: The Next Generation.* A report to the National School Boards Association Council of Urban Boards of Education. Alexandria, Va.: National School Boards Association.

Orfield, Gary, Franklin Monfort, and Melissa Aaron. 1989. *The Status of School Desegregation 1968–1986: Integration and Public Policy—National, State, and Metropolitan Trends in Public Schools.* A report to the National School Boards Association Council of Urban Boards of Education. Alexandria, Va.: National School Boards Association.

Outtz, Janice H. 1993. *The Demographics of American Families.* Washington, D.C.: Institute for Educational Leadership, Center for Demographic Policy.

Payne, Norma J., and Barbara L. Jackson. 1978. "The Status of Black Women in Educational Administration." *Emergent Leadership*, vol. 2(3):1- 17.

Preston, Michael B., Lenneal J. Henderson, and Paul L. Puryear. 1987. *The New Black Politics: The Search for Political Power.* New York: Longman.

Ravitch, Diane. 1974. *The Great School Wars.* New York: Basic Books.

————. 1983. *The Troubled Crusade: American Education 1945–1980*. New York: Basic Books.

Scott, Hugh. 1980. *The Black Superintendent: Messiah or Scapegoat?* Washington, D.C.: Howard University Press.

Sizemore, Barbara. 1986. "The Limits of the Black Superintendency: A Review of the Literature." *Journal of Educational Equity and Leadership*, vol. 6(3):180-203.

Spring, Joel. 1994. *American Education*. New York: McGraw Hill.

The Twentieth Century Fund Task Force on School Governance. 1992. *Facing the Challenge*. New York: The Twentieth Century Fund.

Tyack, David. 1974. *The One Best System: A History of American Urban Education*. Cambridge, Mass.: Harvard University Press.

Tyack, David, and Elisabeth Hansot. 1982. *Managers of Virtue: Public School Leadership in America 1820–1980*. New York: Basic Books.

Tyack, David, Robert Lowe, and Elisabeth Hansot. 1984. *Public Schools in Hard Times: The Great Depression and Recent Years*. Cambridge: Harvard University Press.

U.S. Department of Education, National Center for Education Statistics. 1991a. *Characteristics of the 100 Largest Public Elementary and Secondary School Districts in the U.S., 1988–89*. Washington, DC.: U.S. Government Printing Office.

————. 1991b. "Public Elementary and Secondary Schools and Agencies in the United States and Outlying Areas: School Year 1989–90—April 1991 Final Tabulations, Common Core of Data." Washington, D.C.: U.S. Government Printing Office.

————. 1992. *The Conditions of Education*. Washington, D.C.: U.S. Government Printing Office.

Weeres, Joseph G., and Bruce Cooper. 1991. "Public Policy Perspectives on Urban Schools." In *The Politics of Urban Education in the United States* (The 1991 Yearbook of the Politics of Education Association), edited by James Cibulka, Rodney Reed, and Kenneth Wong. London: The Falmer Press.

Weick, Kenneth E. 1976. "Educational Organizations as Loosely Coupled Systems." *Administrative Science Quarterly*, vol. 21:1-19.

Zeigler, L. Harmon, M. Kent Jennings, and G. Wayne Peak. 1974. *Governing American Schools: Political Interaction in Local School Districts*. North Scituate, Mass.: Duxbury Press.

Zeigler, L. Harmon, Ellen Nehoe, and Jane Reisman. 1985. *City Managers and School Superintendents' Response to Community Conflict*. New York: Praeger.

Interviews

Milton Bins, formerly with The Council of the Great City Schools. Focus group discussion, Washington, D.C., November 20, 1990.

Erma Brooks, former administrative assistant to John O'Bryant, Boston School Committee. Boston, May 20, 1992.

Alonzo Crim, former superintendent, Atlanta Public Schools. Interviewed several times in Atlanta, 1991–92.

LaRuth Gray, associate director, Metropolitan Center, New York University; secretary, Commission of Superintendents, National Alliance of Black School Educators; former superintendent, Abbot Union School District, Irvington, New York. New York City, July 10, 1992.

Betty Hale, Institute for Educational Leadership. Focus group discussion, Washington, D.C., November 20, 1990.

J. Jerome Harris, former superintendent, New York City Community School District No. 13 and Atlanta, Ga. Interviewed several times in New York City and Atlanta, 1991–92.

Lois Harrison-Jones, superintendent, Boston Public Schools. Boston, May 22, 1992.

Rev. Nicholas Hood, Jr., minister, United Church of Christ. Detroit, June 5, 1992.

Rev. Nicholas Hood, Sr., councilman, Detroit City Council. Detroit, June 4, 1992.

Arthur Jefferson, former superintendent, Detroit Public Schools. Detroit, June 4, 1992; numerous telephone interviews, 1991–92.

Barbara McCloud, Joint Center for Political and Economic Studies. Focus group discussion, Washington, D.C., November 20, 1990.

Deborah McGriff, superintendent, Detroit Public Schools. Detroit, June 4, 1992.

Floretta McKenzie, McKenzie Group; former superintendent, Washington, D.C., Public Schools. Washington, D.C., November 20, 1990.

John O'Bryant, former president and member, Boston School Committee. Boston, May 21, 1992.

Paul Parks, chairperson, Boston School Committee. Boston, June 25, 1992.

Lawrence Patrick, member and former president, Detroit School Board. Detroit, June 4, 1992.

Robert Peterkin, director, Urban Superintendents Program, Harvard Graduate School of Education; former superintendent of schools, Milwaukee, Wis., and Cambridge, Mass. Cambridge, June 25, 1992.

Santee Ruffin, vice president for Education Policy and Reform, National Board for Professional Teaching Standards. Detroit, June 4, 1992.

Michael Usdan, president, Institute for Educational Leadership. Focus group discussion, Washington, D.C., November 20, 1990.Appendix

APPENDIX

Table A1
Student Enrollments and Race (Percent Distribution) for Big-City†
School Districts, 1967–68 and 1988–89

School	1967–68			1988–89				
District	Total	White	Black	Total	White	Black	Hisp.	Asian
Anchorage	–	–	–	40,007	–	–	–	–
Atlanta	113,841	41%	59%	63,448	7%	92%	–	–
Baltimore	191,997	36	64	107,486	19	80	*	1%
Boston	91,608	73	26	59,184	24	48	19%	8
Broward City (Fort Lauderdale)	93,777	74	26	142,202	61	29	8	2
Buffalo	73,391	–	–	46,228	42	48	7	1
Chicago	574,801	41	52	410,230	12	60	25	3
Cincinnati	87,706	–	–	51,606	38	61	*	1
Cleveland	152,038	43	56	72,116	23	70	5	1
Columbus	107,413	73	26	65,160	51	46	*	2
Dade City (Miami)	220,011	64	24	268,047	21	33	44	1
Dallas	157,110	63	30	130,904	19	48	31	2
Dayton	59,931	–	–	28,302	37	63	*	*
Denver	94,995	66	14	58,664	35	22	38	3
Detroit	293,000	41	58	181,838	8	89	2	1
East Baton Rouge	61,501	–	–	57,810	44	54	*	1
El Paso	59,476	–	–	63,169	22	5	72	1
Fresno	63,669	–	–	64,446	38	11	33	17
Houston	256,459	54	33	190,290	16	41	41	3
Indianapolis	108,543	–	–	50,214	50	49	1	1
Jacksonville (Duval City)	122,227	–	–	105,269	60	37	1	2

Continued on next page

Table A1 continued

School District	1967–68			1988–89				
	Total	White	Black	Total	White	Black	Hisp.	Asian
Long Beach	73,029	86	7	–	34	19	27	20
Los Angeles	652,508	55	22	592,881	16	17	59	8
Memphis	123,465	48	52	105,628	21	78	*	1
Milwaukee	128,170	73	24	97,294	34	54	8	2
Minneapolis	70,368	–	–	40,024	53%	29%	2%	10%††
Nashville	93,063	76%	30%	68,063	60	37	*	2
New Orleans	108,861	–	–	84,098	34	66	–	–
New York	1,101,804	48	30	936,153	20	38	31	7
Norfolk	56,440	–	–	36,690	38	58	1	3
Oakland	68,571	–	–	51,218	9	59	14	17
Oklahoma City	73,967	–	–	38,736	47	39	7	3††
Omaha	61,397	–	–	41,143	67	27	4	1
Philadelphia	279,907	40	58	191,141	24	63	9	4
Phoenix	25,960	–	–	18,736	45	14	36	2
Pittsburgh	76,215	–	–	39,809	47	52	*	1
Portland	78,664	–	–	53,130	73	16	2	7
Rochester	45,594	–	–	31,774	29	54	14	2
Sacramento	52,741	–	–	46,632	–	–	–	–
St. Louis	123,917	–	–	46,128	22	77	*	1
St. Paul	47,814	–	–	33,457	61	16	6	17
San Diego	118,934	–	–	117,168	41	16	23	19
San Francisco	99,373	42	26	65,528	15	19	19	47
Seattle	94,441	–	–	43,023	47	24	5	21
Toledo	66,336	–	–	41,978	58	37	5	1
Tucson	52,091	68	5	56,520	56	6	33	2
Washington, DC	148,911	8	92	84,792	4	91	4	1

Note: A dash indicates the data were not available.

* Less than 0.5 percent.

† Defined as districts belonging to The Council of the Great City Schools.

†† Native Americans.

Source: Figures for 1988–89 from The Council of the Great City Schools and National Center for Education Statistics. Figures for 1967–68 from Gary Orfield, Franklin Monfort, and Melissa Aaron, *The Status of School Desegregation, 1968–1986.*

Table A2
Gender/Minority Characteristics of Superintendents of Schools, 1987–88 and 1989–90

	1987–88	1989–90	
	Percent	Number	Percent
Total		11,356	
Women*	4%	515	5%
Men*	96	10,831	95
Minority**	3	9,844	3

Comment: The percentage of superintendents who are women shows a slight increase betweeen 1988 and 1990, reflecting similar gradual increases throughout the 1980s. The percentage who are minorities, however, changed very little between 1988 and 1990.

* Number of women and men superintendents reported for 40 states and the District of Columbia.

** Number of racial minorities reported for 36 states and the District of Columbia. Minorities include American Indian, Asian/Pacific Islander, Black, and Hispanic ethnicity.   ·

Source: American Association of School Administrators, Office of Minority Affairs, *Women and Minorities in School Administration: Facts and Figures 1989–90*, p. 4.

Table A3
Minority Superintendents: Percent of Total, by Race/Ethnic Group, 1987–88 and 1989–90

	1987–88	1989–90
Minority, total	3.1%	3.4%
American Indian	0.3	0.4
Asian/Pacific	0.1	0.2
Black	1.2	1.6
Hispanic	1.5	1.2
White	96.9	96.6
Total	**100.0**	**100.0**

Source: American Association of School Administrators, Office of Minority Affairs, *Women and Minorities in School Administration: Facts and Figures 1989–90*, p. 5.

Table A4
Minority Superintendents: Number and Percent by Race/Ethnic Group, for Gender Categories, 1989–90*

	Women	Men	Total
All	434	8,549	8,983
	4.8%	95.2%	100%
American Indian	3	38	41
	0.0%	0.4%	0.4%
Asian / Pacific Islanders	7	7	14
	0.1%	0.1%	0.2%
Black	22	120	142
	0.2%	1.3%	1.5%
Hispanic	5	113	118
	0.1%	1.3%	1.4%
Mixed / Other	0	0	0
	0.0%	0.0%	0.0%
White	397	8,270	8,667
	4.4%	92.1%	96.5%

* Excludes states that do not report data by gender and race.

Source: American Association of School Administrators, Office of Minority Affairs, *Women and Minorities in School Administration: Facts and Figures 1989–90*, pp. 4, 5, 14.

Table A5
Race and Gender of Big-City* Superintendents, by Year of Appointment and District, 1982–92

Year	School District	Black	White	Hispanic	Gender
1982	Philadelphia	X			F
	San Diego		X		M
1984	Omaha		X		M
1985	New Orleans	X			M
	Oklahoma City		X		M
1986	Long Beach		X		M
	Seattle		X		M
1987	E. Baton Rouge		X		M
1988	Dallas	X			M
	Minneapolis		X		M
1989	Buffalo	X			M
	Chicago	X			M
	Jacksonville		X		M
	Sacramento	X			M
1990	Anchorage		X		M
	Atlanta	X			M
	Broward County		X		M
	Dade County			X	M
	Denver	X			F
	Los Angeles			X	M
	New York City			X	M
	Oakland			X	M
	Phoenix		X		M
	St. Louis		X		M
	Toledo	X			M

* Defined as districts belonging to The Council of the Great City Schools.

Continued on next page

Table A5 continued

Year	School District	Black	White	Hispanic	Gender
1991	Baltimore	x			M
	Boston	x			F
	Cincinnati		x		M
	Columbus	x			M
	Dayton	x			M
	Detroit	x			F
	El Paso			x	M
	Houston		x		M
	Indianapolis	x			M
	Milwaukee	x			M
	St. Paul	x			M
	Tucson			x	M
	Washington DC	x			M
1992	Cleveland	x			F
	Memphis	x			F
	Norfolk		x		M
	Pittsburgh		x		F
	Fresno		x		M
	Rochester			x	M
	Portland		x		M
	San Francisco			x	M
	Nashville		x		M

Source: The Council of the Great City Schools.

Table A6
Number of Big-City* Superintendents, by Race and Gender, 1992

	Black	White	Hispanic	Total
Female	6	1	0	7
Male	14	18	8	40
Total	20	19	8	47

* Defined as districts belonging to The Council of the Great City Schools.
Source: The Council of the Great City Schools.

Table A7
Number of Recently Appointed Minority Superintendents of Big-City* School Districts, by Year of Appointment, 1982–92

Year	Number	
1982	2	
1983	–	
1984	–	
1985	2	(1 announced retirement)
1986	2	(1 announced retirement)
1987	–	
1988	2	
1989	4	
1990	11	
1991	13	
1992	9	(1 interim)

* Defined as districts belonging to The Council of the Great City Schools.
Source: The Council of the Great City Schools.

INDEX

Names and titles of persons, places, organizations, legislation, and court rulings.

Balancing Act:
The Political Role of the Urban School Superintendent
by Barbara L. Jackson

Editing and proofreading: Marc DeFrancis, Peter Slavin

Word processing: Glynda Featherstone

Text and cover design: Theresa Kilcourse

Formatting: Theresa Kilcourse, Linda M. Cunningham (EEI, Inc.)

Joint Center for Political and Economic Studies

OTHER JOINT CENTER
BOOKS OF INTEREST

Economic Perspectives on Affirmative Action
edited by Margaret Simms

The Declining Economic Status of Black Children:
Examining the Change
by Cynthia Rexroat

The Congressional Black Caucus in the 103rd Congress
by David Bositis

Young Black Males in Jeopardy: Risk Factors and
*Intervention Strategies**
by Alex Poinsett and Margaret Simms

For ordering information, call University Press of America at
1-800-462-6420.

---

* For ordering information, call the Joint Center at 202-789-3500.